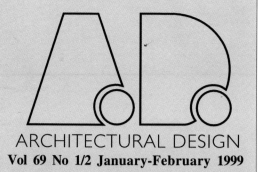

ARCHITECTURAL DESIGN
Vol 69 No 1/2 January-February 1999

EDITORIAL OFFICES:
42 LEINSTER GARDENS, LONDON W2 3AN
TEL: + 44 171 262 5097 FAX: + 44 171 262 5093

EDITOR: Maggie Toy
DEPUTY EDITOR: Ellie Duffy
EDITORIAL ASSISTANT: Bob Fear
DESIGN: Mario Bettella and Andrea Bettella/Artmedia
ADVERTISEMENT SALES: Nicky Douglas

CONSULTANTS: Catherine Cooke, Terry Farrell, Kenneth
Frampton, Charles Jencks, Heinrich Klotz, Leon Krier,
Robert Maxwell, Demetri Porphyrios, Kenneth Powell,
Colin Rowe, Derek Walker

SUBSCRIPTION OFFICES:

UK: JOHN WILEY & SONS LTD
JOURNALS ADMINISTRATION DEPARTMENT
1 OAKLANDS WAY, BOGNOR REGIS
WEST SUSSEX, PO22 9SA, UK
TEL: 01243 843272 FAX: 01243 843232
E-mail: cs-journals@wiley.co.uk

USA AND CANADA:
JOHN WILEY & SONS, INC
JOURNALS ADMINISTRATION DEPARTMENT
605 THIRD AVENUE
NEW YORK, NY 10158
TEL: + 1 212 850 6645 FAX: + 1 212 850 6021
CABLE JONWILE TELEX: 12-7063
E-mail: subinfo@wiley.com

ANNUAL SUBSCRIPTION RATES 1999: UK £135.00 (institutional
rate), £90.00 (personal rate); Outside UK US$225.00 (institu-
tional rate), $145.00 (personal rate). AD is published six times a
year. Prices are for six issues and include postage and handling
charges. Periodicals postage paid at Jamaica, NY 11431. Air freight
and mailing in the USA by Publications Expediting Services Inc,
200 Meacham Ave, Elmont, Long Island, NY 11003.

SINGLE ISSUES: UK £18.99; Outside UK $29.95. Order two or
more titles and postage is free. For orders of one title please add
£2.00/$5.00. To receive order by air please add £5.50/$10.00.

POSTMASTER: send address changes to AD, c/o Publications
Expediting Services Inc, 200 Meacham Ave, Elmont, Long
Island, NY 11003.

Printed in Italy. All prices are subject to change without notice.
[ISSN: 0003-8504]

CONTENTS

ARCHITECTURAL DESIGN **MAGAZINE**

Architectural Design,
September 1966

ARCHITECTURAL DESIGN **PROFILE** NO 137

DES-RES ARCHITECTURE

Chance de Silva Architects,
Venus, London

Claudio Silvestrin,
Riverside One Apartment,
London

LOOKING BACK, LOOKING FORWARD

The articles, 'Living, 1990' and 'Just a Few Chairs and a House', which appeared in *AD* in the late 1960s (March 1967 and September 1966 respectively), addressed the issue of domesticity and architecture in terms that are surprisingly relevant today. In the first, Warren Chalk of Archigram projected a vision of the house of the future: 'The only way to involve the public in architecture is to give them what they want. We see self-selection as the obvious solution'; while Peter Smithson, in 'Just a Few Chairs and a House', looked back over 20 or so years to evaluate the impact of the work of Charles and Ray Eames: 'by the late 1950s the Eames way of seeing things had in a sense become everybody's style'.

Sandwiched between adverts for asbestos-cement for multi-storey construction and heavy-duty vinyl wall coverings, the double-page spread of Archigram's house of the 1990s (reproduced overleaf) – a project also exhibited at Harrods department store in London in March 1967 – was a lighthearted attempt to predict the impact of technology on the house of the future: 'A fully integrated systems approach to domestic bliss', as Warren Chalk wrote in his description of the project;

Architecture lies well outside the orbis of technological forecasting – the ability to look further ahead than you can see – but inevitably and eventually it will be pressurized into a more receptive position. Such thoughts from the early days of the microchip provide an interesting perspective from which to view the diverse collection of contemporary house projects brought together in this issue.

'Just a Few Chairs and a House', Peter Smithson's retrospective tribute to Charles and Ray Eames, was published in a special 'Eames Celebration' issue of *AD* in September 1966. In this article, which is reproduced opposite, Peter Smithson defined the 'Eames-aesthetic' as a kind of break-away development from the modernist 'machine-aesthetic', an idea he introduced through a discussion of the role of chair design as a 'forward-runner' of design change

The enduring influence of both the Eames partnership and Archigram group on the aesthetics of domesticity and on perceptions of the house lies with their understanding of technology – forecasting in the case of Archigram, technology transfer from the work of Charles and Ray Eames. In applying manufacturing

technology already available in America in the late 1940s to the domestic sphere (House at Santa Monica Canyon, 1949), the Eames' were following in the tradition of the Modern Movement. But, as Peter Smithson pointed out, what made the 'Eames-aesthetic' different from the 'machine-aesthetic' was a factor he defined as 'extra-cultural surprise'; the 'wide-eyed wonder' of reinterpretation through acute observation.

The fact that the Eames' work remains an enduring influence on the aesthetics of the house is perhaps due to their acute observation of the subtle difference between the domestication of the industrial (which is what they achieved), and the industrialisation of the domestic (which is what they managed to avoid).

Ellie Duffy

JUST A FEW CHAIRS AND A HOUSE

AN ESSAY ON THE EAMES-AESTHETIC

Peter Smithson, AD *September 1966*

In the 1950s the whole design climate was permanently changed by the work of Charles and Ray Eames. By a few chairs and a house.

Now chairs have always been the forward-runners of design-change. They have for some mysterious reason the capacity of establishing a new sense of style almost overnight.

Rietveld established a whole new design mode with a chair. So did Mackintosh with his.

In the 1950s the Eames' moved design away from the machine-aesthetic and bicycle technology, on which it had lived since the 1920s, into the world of the cinema-eye and the technology of the production aircraft; from the world of the painters into the world of the layout men.

In a sense both the machine-aesthetic and the Eames-aesthetic are art-forms of ordinary life and ordinary objects seen with an eye that sees the ordinary as also magical.[1]

The machine-aesthetic selected with care those objects from ordinary life that were based on simple geometries – on cones, on spheres, on 'engineers' profiles'; objects whose commonality was composable, ie pictures could be made from their arrangement and out of which an art-discipline could be erected.[2]

The Eames-aesthetic, made definitive in the House at Santa Monica Canyon, California, 1949 (as the machine-aesthetic was given canonical form in the 'dwelling unit' in the Esprit Nouveau Pavilion, Decorative Arts Exposition, in Paris, 1925), is based on an equally careful selection but with extra-cultural surprise, rather than harmony of profile, as its criteria. A kind of wide-eyed wonder of seeing the culturally disparate together and so happy with each other. This sounds like whimsy but the basic vehicle – the steel lattice frame and in the case of the house, the colour film and colour processing in the graphics work, the pressings and mouldings in the case of the furniture – is ordinary to the culture.

And this is what separates the Eames' 'selection and juxtaposition' technique from neo-Victorian screen-making and pop art forms of either the Barbara Jones or Peter Blake sorts.

Charles Eames is a natural Californian Man using his native resources and know-how of the film-making, the aircraft and the advertising industries – as others drink water; that is almost without thinking. And it is this combination of expertise, and the availability of the expertise of others, which produces the apparent casualness that is special to the American life-form and its art-form.[3] (Bad Day at Black Rock is of the same period, ie mid-1950s.)

And, as it is the California Man's real originality to accept the clean and pretty as normal, it is not surprising that it is the Eames' who have made it respectable to like pretty things. This seems extraordinary, but in our old world, pretty things are usually equated with social irresponsibility. That we can be persuaded to accept the pretty is because their work is by no means without a sense of law. When we say 'that's a very Eames Photograph' we all know what it means. It is a special way of looking at things, a special sort of composition. It communicates a love of the object photographed, a kind of reverence for the object's integrity. The Eames-aesthetic is to do with object-integrity. This is what gives their whole output cohesion.

Before Eames, no chairs (of the modern canon) were many coloured, or really light in weight, or not fundamentally rectangular in plan (ie the chairs of Rietveld, Stam, Breuer, Le Corbusier, Mies, Aalto).

Eames' chairs are the first chairs which can be put into any position in an empty room. They look as if they had alighted there – that crow in the wheelchair photograph is no coincidence, the chair belongs to the occupants not to the building.

(Mies chairs are especially of the building and not of the occupants. Maybe what worries one about the Eames library-chair-with-footstool is that it is a reversion to the club-chair – immovably part of the Club.)

The Eames chairs of the new canon are more like the pre-Courrèges clothes of the occupants; pretty, light, non-geometric, apparently casual. They use nylon, stretch vinyl, fibreglass reinforced plastic, all of which can be self-coloured, and which carry no overtones of furniture from other cultures.

They use aluminium castings and wire-struts which remind one (but only if one thinks about it) of new and old aeroplanes, not of other furniture.

A lot of energy has been poured into their detail; it is workmanlike, explicit, even eloquent, but it is quiet. They can be photographed as a fragment, they can be enjoyed as a fragment. They have a high object-integrity.

When the Santa Monica house was first published, Europeans assumed its look of fragility was a consequence of being able to not worry about weather problems in an equable climate. But in reality it is stoutly built, and equipped to bourgeois standards. Its lightness, its flicker of change, is its style.

And by the late 1950s the Eames way of seeing things had in a sense become everybody's style.

Notes

1 This sounds like a description of the role of holiday film as myth-maker to America.
2 See Ozenfant's *The Foundations of Modern Art.*
3 And is presumably why Zen is so popular on the West Coast (?).

1

2

Living, 1990

Archigram Group

The intention of this exhibit, sponsored by the *Weekend Telegraph* on show this month at Harrods in Knightsbridge, is to demonstrate how computer technology and concepts of expendability and personal leisure might influence the form of future homes.

The living space 1, 4, is intended to be in a space frame 2 or suspended within a tensegrity structure. Enclosure is created by skins which close together or separate electronically. The floor and ceiling can be transformed from hard to soft as acoustic/space/light regulators or inflated in certain areas as required for reclining and sleeping. The adjustable screens of the robot towers (robots Fred and James) 8, define smaller areas within the main volume where one can be totally enclosed—enveloped in an event generated by the projection of films, light, sound and smellies. The push of a button or a spoken command, a bat of an eyelid will set these transformations in motion—providing what you want where and when you need it 10–16. Each member of a family will choose what they want—the shape and layout of their spaces, their activities or what have you. The hover chairs 1, 9, will provide an instant link-up with local amenities or access to the nearest transit interchange. A fully integrated systems approach to domestic bliss.

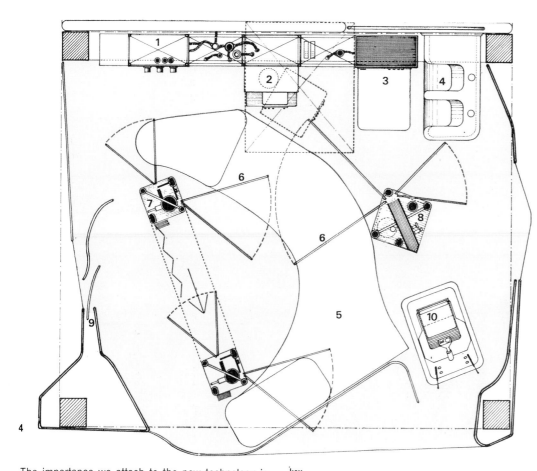

3

5

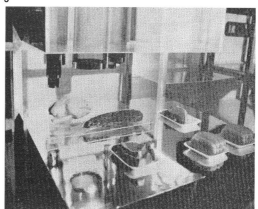

6

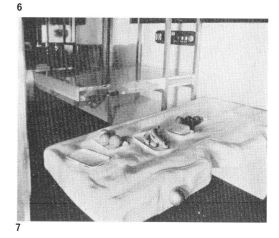

7

4

The importance we attach to the new technology is quite clear. To say that electronics is important to the future of architecture is a truism—something to talk about and discuss, yet feel unable to produce constructive and significant propositions about. This vision of the dwelling of the future takes an elementary and popularized form, but it is not a compromise. It makes clear, without any falsification of our beliefs, ideas that are otherwise difficult to grasp. Participation in an event such as this helps to redefine the problems we recognize to be important; clarifies our position before another step is taken. It might enable all of us to endure better the crisis we live in. Architecture remains well outside the orbit of technological forecasting—the ability to look ahead further than you can see—but inevitably and eventually it will be pressurized into a more receptive position. The public is not interested in the current betrayal of the Bauhaus achievement; it is equally, reluctant to suffer the inefficiencies of Welfare State housing. The only way to involve the public in architecture is to give them what they want. We see self-selection as the obvious solution.
Warren Chalk

key

1 hardware dispenser	6 3D TV screens
2 food dispenser	7 robot 'Fred'
3 master control	8 robot 'James'
4 inflatable bench	9 screen
5 inflatable couch	10 hoverchair

Photos: 1, 6, & 7 Terence Donovan courtesy Weekend Telegraph; *5 Archigram Group*

8

9

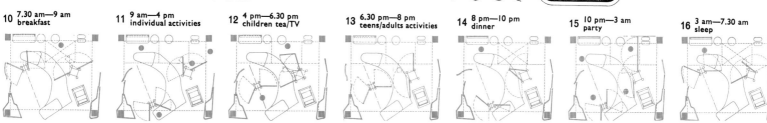

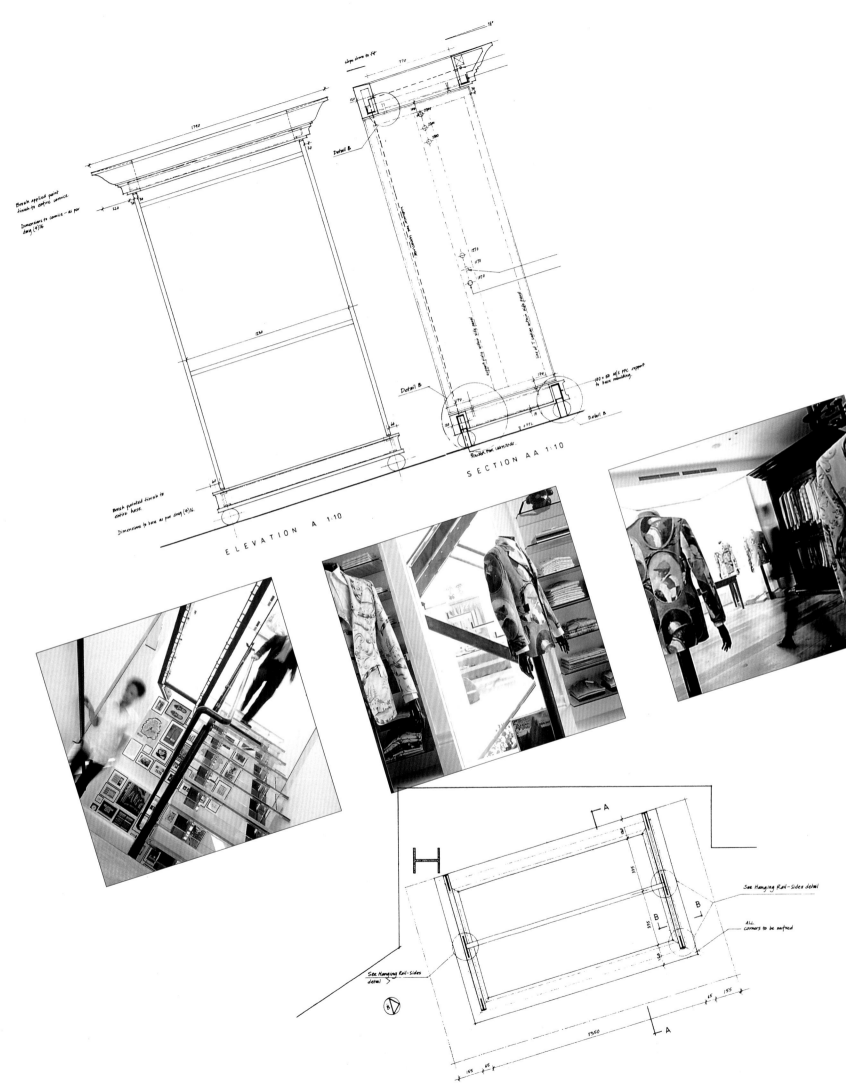

SOPHIE HICKS ARCHITECTS
WESTBOURNE HOUSE
London

Domesticity is the theme behind 'Westbourne House', the shop in Westbourne Grove, Notting Hill, created for fashion designer Paul Smith by architect Sophie Hicks. The architectural practice was involved in all aspects of the design, from structural rebuilding – gutting the interior, inserting an exposed steel structure to pin back the brick and stucco facades, and introducing a top-lit central stair in raw steel and glass – to the design of fittings, and the sourcing of antiques for adaptation.

Distributed over three floors of what was once a Victorian family house, the shop interior is generated by the abstraction of residential traditions: display cases are converted from such icons of domesticity as picture frames, dining tables, wardrobes and dressers.

Through a subtle subversion of the traditional, these objects have been designed to create a subliminal impression of home in the shop, while at the same time evoking a somewhat surreal atmosphere: the frames that hang on the walls display not ancestral portraits, but Paul Smith accessories; a wardrobe clad in grey velvet 'floats' in an upstairs room, occasional floorboards are replaced by glass 'planks', and a vast refectory table is set not for supper, but with leather goods, watches and pens under glass.

TEMPORARY BUILDING
WALL STREET, NEW YORK
Lisa Tilder

Wall Street is the location of one of the original fortification walls of New Amsterdam (New York). Throughout the city's history Wall Street has been the centre of New York's financial district. With the digitalisation of the stock exchange it is now also the heart of the city's electronic community.

This project for a temporary community centre at the eastern end of Wall Street was developed in response to a competition sponsored by the Van Alen Institute of New York. The project addresses the juxtaposition of the notion of the wall as a physical boundary in a district of the city dominated by electronic space. The temporary community structure was formed in response to transformations of use that are taking place in the district – from a strictly business location operating from nine to five, to a 24-hour mixed-use locality, with residential spaces and studios for multi media companies now also characterising the district .

The temporary building begins as a recognisable wall but transforms into a series of volumes which shift to accommodate immediate needs. The evolved wall consists of individual glass display panels which slide to accept varying volumes of activity and space. The entire building is designed to evolve and relocate as new forms of communication between street, site and community become possible. In this project, the wall as fixed barrier transforms to become a fluid and transparent mediator.

Lisa Tilder is a practising architect and Assistant Professor of Architecture at The Austin E Knowlton School of Architecture, The Ohio State University. Her work explores the critical relationship between technology, architecture and culture in various media, from interactive constructions and installations to competition entries and small building projects. She is currently working with QuickTime Virtual Reality technologies to create interactive three-dimensional representations of space.

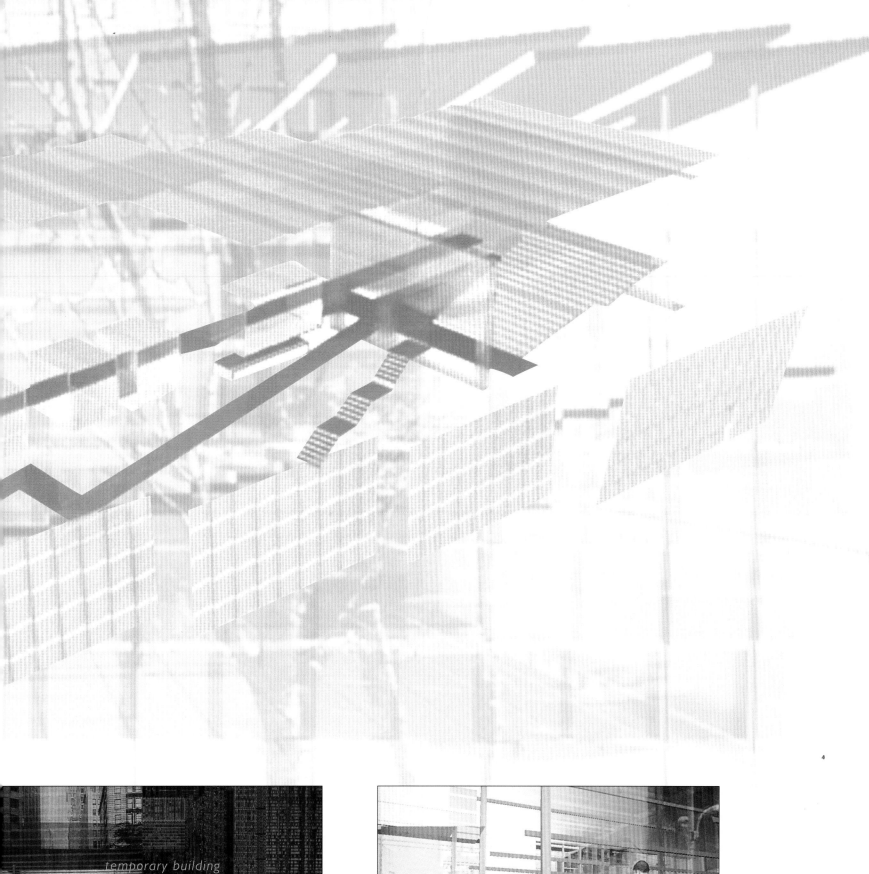

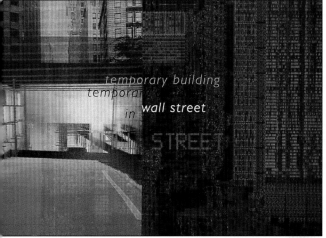

temporary building
tempora
in wall street
STREET

SKYLINER

Exhibitions

MODERN BRITAIN, 1929–1939

Design Museum, London
20 January – 6 June 1999

This exhibition illustrates the diversity of art and architectural works that emerged during a time of much instablity and economic depression in Britain. In their quest to convey the spirit of innovation that characterises the pre-war Modern Movement, the curators of the exhibition have brought together a broad selection of architectural drawings and photographs, paintings, posters, film, textiles, ceramics, sculpture and furniture. The exhibition has been designed by Sir Norman Foster in collaboration with Danish graphic designer Per Arnoldi.

Images of works by architects such as Berthold Lubetkin – responsible for the Penguin Pool at London Zoo and Highpoint Flats – are thus able to be appreciated in a wider context, enhanced by the unusual cow-hide chairs that graced his own apartment. During this time, and in true Modernist spirit, many architects chose to experiment with other disciplines and to exploit new materials and techniques; creating, for example, chrome and plywood furniture, rugs and bakelite radios, which are all part of the exhibition.

Among the architects whose works are featured in the survey of domestic architecture are Goodhart-Rendel (St Olaf House), Ernö Goldfinger (Willow Road flats) and Wells Coates (Lawn Road flats). Social issues were obviously very much at the forefront of the design industries, and this is communicated by the variety of health centres, educational projects and buildings for the leisure industry that were built during this perod.

FROM ABOVE: Berthold Lubetkin/Tecton, Highpoint One, London, 1933–35; Tecton, Finsbury Health Centre, London, 1935–38; Berthold Lubetkin/Tecton, penthouse, Highpoint Two, London, 1937–38; Marcel Breuer, dining table, 1936; Wells Coates, Ekco Radio, 1934

Reviews

Books

The Georgian Country House: Architecture, Landscape and Society by Dana Arnold, *Sutton Publishing (Stroud), 1998, 224pp, colour and b/w ills, HB £25.00*

The country house was a focal point of Georgian architecture, landscape and society. This book, published concurrently with the following titles, explores the meaning of this distinct architectural form through a wide range of examples and approaches to its history. The main body of the text presents an analysis of the social and cultural significance of the country house, complemented by essays from experts in a variety of disciplines. A wealth of illustrations, showing exteriors, interiors and landscapes of houses ranging from Blenheim and Harewood to lesser known examples such as A la Ronde, provides one of the most historical and visual surveys of the period.

The Georgian Country House offers the reader new interpretations and seeks to provide an insight into the pivotal role of the country house played in eighteenth- and early nineteenth-century society. The volume begins with an examination of developments in the architecture and planning of the country house and its estate, moving on to unravel contemporary interpretations of the house through its appearance in literature; the role of women in the design of the country house; and its uses as a centre for entertainment and hospitality.

Later chapters deal with the significance of antiquity and the extent to which the Grand Tour influenced collections; the relationship between the town house and the country house; changes in farming practices and the lasting effect that more progressive methods had upon both the landscape of the country house and the social relationship which it encouraged, as well as Richard Payne Knight's suggestion of an alternative to the landscape parks of Capability Brown.

The Georgian Villa edited by Dana Arnold, *Sutton Publishing (Stroud), 1998, 192pp, b/w ills, PB £12.99*

The villa remains one of the most potent architectural forms in Western culture; the idea of a cultural retreat for relaxation and contemplation having endured from antiquity up to the present day. Yet there have been many changes in its structure and use following the social and economic circumstances of its owners, many of which took place during the Georgian period.

This stimulating book brings together a number of leading historians to investigate the eighteenth-century villa in its wider context. Images of the villa – real or imagined – are shown to reveal much about contemporary attitudes.

The role of Andrea Palladio is re-examined in relation his influence on architects throughout the period, including such key figures as Colen Campbell, the architect of Stourhead in Wiltshire and Mereworth in Kent, and the well-established patron/architect Lord Burlington, whose villa in Chiswick (designed to house his collection of paintings and artefacts) remains one of the most austere examples of the period.

The range of form, planning and sources of the villa is evident not only in the proliferation of designs by Robert Adam but also in the variations of the villa that exist north of the border, for example in Edinburgh and Glasgow, where it provided a balanced contrast between city and retreat. Later in the period, changes effected by the demand for new houses and in the urban fabric brought the villa into the city where its elitist aspirations were replaced by democratising principles.

Polite Landscapes by Tom Williamson, *Sutton Publishing (Gloucestershire), 1998, 192pp, b/w ills, PB £12.99*

In this interesting study, Tom Williamson looks at parks and gardens from the perspective of the social historian, thereby providing an insight into the creation of these important features of the eighteenth-century landscape.

Parks and gardens in this era are usually seen as works of art devised by individual geniuses such as Capability Brown and Humphrey Repton. However, Williamson argues that the gentry who paid for these private landscapes, and lived in them, were motivated by more complex interests and needs. The appearance of gentlemen's pleasure grounds reflects changing attitudes to politics, society and much else. Parks and gardens were homes, farms and forestry enterprises, as well as being pictures: their form was moulded by the needs of hunting, riding and other recreational activities as much as by the writings of philosophers and aesthetes.

This fully-illustrated survey includes contemporary maps and plans in addition to a broad selection of paintings and photographs. The text makes interesting reading for anyone with an enthusiasm for gardens, parks, great houses and the English landscape.

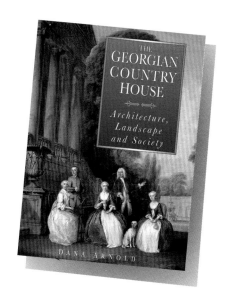

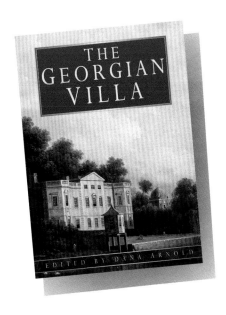

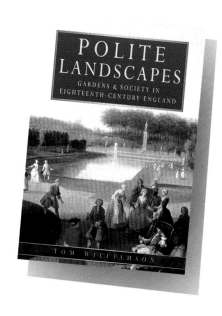

Reviews

Books

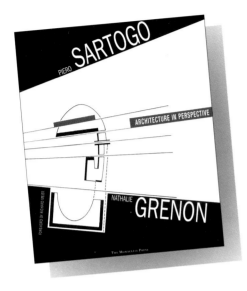

Architecture in Perspective, *by Piero Sartogo Nathalie Grenon, The Monacelli Press (New York), 1998, 190pp, b/w ills, PB £27.00*

Piero Sartogo and Nathalie Grenon are, as described by Richard Meier in the foreword, 'European Architects with a world perspective'. This volume clearly demonstrates that point of view and is the first to cover the work of this Rome- and New York-based architectural practice.

It includes more than 30 projects – built, unbuilt, and under construction – from around the world (the United States, Italy, France, Spain, Switzerland, Wales, Japan and Taiwan). These are organised in reverse chronological order and illuminated by critiques and essays by such leading architectural writers as Rudolf Arnheim, Bruno Zevi, Paul Goldberger, and Kenneth Frampton. This unique organisation creates an intense dialogue between architectural criticism and built form.

The book opens with the new Italian Embassy in Washington, DC. Currently under construction, this building is Sartogo and Grenon's most important project in the United States. Other significant New York projects featured are the Italian Trade Centre and the Banca di Roma, both located in midtown Manhattan. In addition, the book covers urban planning projects, important international competitions, product design, installations for both exhibitions and expositions, and Sartogo's seminal early projects, the Gescal Public Housing Development in Milan and the Medical Association Building in Rome.

Throughout all their work, as Sartogo writes in the introduction, these international architects constantly perceive new ways to design 'conceptual space – the dimension beyond reality . . . that lives within the physical structure of rooms and buildings and needs to be articulated'.

TEN Arquitectos: Work in Progress, *by Enrique Norten and Bernardo Gomez-Pimienta, The Monacelli Press (New York), 1998, 221pp, colour and b/w ills, PB £25.00*

This monograph features a selection of 21 buildings and projects by the practice. While the chronological presentation offers an analysis of the development of TEN Arquitectos, it also sets out to emphasise the partners' view of each design as both a point of culmination and departure, informing successive schemes.

Included in the selection of buildings – almost all of which are located in Mexico City – are two major projects for TELEVISA, the largest television network in Mexico; the spectacular National School of Theatre; commercial and retail projects; and a series of remarkable private residences. Also featured are the firm's first projects in the United States: the Nursing and Biomedical Sciences Building at the University of Texas in Houston; a renovation and addition to the College of Architecture at the University of Michigan; Addams Hall and Fine Arts buildings at the University of Pennsylvania in Philadelphia; and the El Camino Real Heritage Centre in Socorro, New Mexico.

The Houses of McKim, Mead & White, *by Samuel G White, photographs by Jonathan Wallen, Thames & Hudson (London), 1998, colour ills, HB £42.00*

This is the first book to focus on the residential work of McKim, Mead & White, one of Americas best known, most prolific and influential architecture firms.

In counterpoint to the Chicago school, who chose a functional, straightforward architectural vocabulary that anticipated modernism, McKim, Mead & White looked back to American colonial architecture, the Renaissance and the French Beaux-Arts tradition for inspiration. Based in New York and with nearly one thousand commissions executed between 1879 and 1912, their work included some of the most prestigious projects of the era: they were responsible for the redesign of the White House and the Mall in Washington DC, the State Capitol of Rhode Island, the campuses of Harvard and Columbia Universities, the Boston Public Library, and the Piperpoint Morgan Library in New York.

However, these monumental projects were only a part of McKim, Mead & White's architectural output; they also lent their sophisticated style to domestic architecture, building splendid summer cottages in Newport and throughout Long Island and the Hudson Valley, in addition to sumptuous town houses in Boston, Baltimore and New York. These projects were built for the most powerful figures of this age, including the Vanderbilts, Whitneys, Pulitzers.

Twenty-eight houses are presented, several shown for the first time and each elegantly recorded with lavish new colour photographs. The works are analysed by Samuel G White, Fellow of the American Institute of Architects. As a practising architect and a great-grandson of Stanford White, he brings a unique perspective to these houses to which he has been given unprecedented access.

Reviews Books

Michael Sorkin Studio: Wiggle, *by Michael Sorkin, The Monacelli Press (New York), 1998, 192pp, colour ills, PB £45.00*

As architecture critic for the *Village Voice*, Michael Sorkin established a reputation as a brilliant – if often irreverent – observer of contemporary culture. While Sorkin's writings such as *Exquisite Corpse* and *Variations on a Theme Park* have become classics in the field of architectural theory and the productions of the Studio have enjoyed international coverage, *Michael Sorkin Studio: Wiggle* is the first comprehensive volume documenting this symbiosis.

In equal parts social commentary, visionary urban design, wry architecture, and polemical performance art, this monograph documents over a decade's worth of projects produced by this important New York-based firm. Although urban areas are most frequently the subject of the Studio's iconoclastic rejuvenation, an attention to nature and natural form is nevertheless ubiquitous.

From the biomorphic Governor's Island proposal to the unabashed representationalism of the Beached Houses, from the luminescent tubers of the Miira installation to the neurological networks of the Neurasia project, the Studio combats the sprawl of automobile-centric urbanism with a decidedly organic vocabulary. In the able hands of the Michael Sorkin Studio, progressive strategies of urban intervention and biological reinjection – as attested to by Tokyo's Godzilla and the East New York projects – are given innovative architectural form.

20th Century Architecture: The Structures that Shaped the Century, *by Jonathan Glancey, Carlton Books Ltd (London), 1998, colour ills, HB £29.95*

Why should architecture be appreciated by, and restricted to, only those who have studied the subject? The culture of the 90s has increased our taste for stylish living, stylish discussion and stylish knowledge. There is no reason why the taste of Mr Average, the ordinary citizen, should not extend to an awareness of the climate – and structures – in which we live, work and socialise.

20th Century Architecture is not a technical manual but an enjoyable read; a taster into the enlightening world of architecture and a picture book that speaks volumes about many of the creations the 20th century has borne, and which we have taken for granted. This volume is about breaking barriers, exploding myths and creating discovery zones for anyone interested in understanding architecture at a personal, social or academic level.

Every major architectural movement is neatly built into *20th Century Architecture* – Arts and Crafts, Classicism, Organic design, Modernism, Postmodernism, Robotic design, and urban design – as is every relevant architect, including Sir Edwin Lutyens, Frank Lloyd Wright, Richard Rogers, Berthold Lubetkin and Charles Rennie Mackintosh. It also envisions future possibilities for the art and science of architecture.

The book also offers interesting historical insights. It exposes, for example, the way in which Nazi and Stalinist influences helped mould designs such as the Reich Chancellery in Berlin and Lomonosov State University in Moscow; how 'the most offensive of the modern atrocities' (namely the Hoover Building in London) has stood the test of time; and suggests that Le Corbusier 'is arguably the century's greatest architect . . . [who] tried harder than almost anyone to give a new shape to a new age'. Design students and general readers alike will be fascinated by this informatively written and beautifully presented work.

Morningside Heights: A History of its Architecture & Development, *by Andrew S Dolkart, Columbia University Press (New York), 1998, 505pp, b/w ills, HB £39.95*

These days, the Morningside Heights area of New York City is known for its distinguished institutions and their fabulous architecture: Columbia University, the Cathedral of St John the Divine, Riverside Church and the Jewish Theological Seminary, to name a few. How did such a spectacular mix of beauty and intellectual function develop on this high plateau in Upper Manhattan?

In this lavishly illustrated book, renowned architectural historian Andrew S Dolkart explores the history of these complexes and of the surrounding residential neighbourhood that later became a blueprint for much of the city's middle-class housing. By tracing the successes and failures of each building project that transformed a rural, outlying area into 'the Acropolis of New York', *Morningside Heights* reveals a fascinating – and until now, untold – chapter in the life of New York City.

Legacies for the Future: Contemporary Architecture in Islamic Societies *edited by Cynthia Davidson, Thames & Hudson ltd, (London), 1998, 175pp, colour ills, PB £16.95*

As a result of the rapidly changing tastes and styles of Western culture, the most highly

Reviews

Books

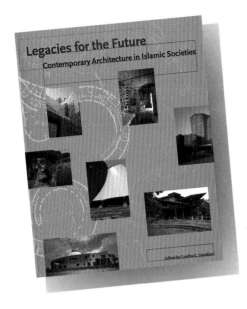

acclaimed architectural designs are often unconnected to the social and cultural contexts from which they spring.

In contrast, in Islamic societies around the world, architecture often plays a far more responsible role, responding to the immediate needs of local and personal exigencies. Consequently, some of the most humanist contemporary architecture is overlooked by the fashions of today's' international design periodicals.

The Aga Khan Award for Architecture was established in 1977 in order to bring global attention to the work of architects and designers in the Muslim world. With an international jury made up of Western and non-Western experts and architects, it has helped foster a greater understanding of architecture in developing countries. Previous winners of the Award include a number of internationally acclaimed architects, such as Balkrishna Doshi, Ken Yeang, Jean Nouvel, Louis Khan, Henning Larsen and Hassan Fathy.

Living on the Water, *by Elizabeth McMillian, Thames & Hudson (London), 1998, 192pp, colour ills, HB £24.95*

'Our world provides many evocative watery settings and, like human beings since the dawn of time, we continue to gravitate towards sites like these for the beauty and experience of nature that they provide.'

In this volume, Elizabeth McMillian defines part of the appeal which encourages us to exist near water and demonstrates the special properties of the locations she has chosen with luscious photographs and brief project descriptions. These encompass an incredible range of sumptuous homes from around the world, all of which are located near water.

Drawing on the spiritual and purifying power of water, architectural designers throughout the ages have used its elusive reflective properties to create spaces and places of peace and tranquillity. From the majestic temples of the far East to the riverside log cabins of North America, the principles of water association are used in similar ways.

The worldwide focus of this book conveys the variety of forms in which settling by water can be manifested. Throughout the volume, the reader is presented with an extremely impressive range of high-quality photographs.

The selection of projects comprises a catalogue of desirable vacations and permanent residences in some of the world's most glamorous settings. Evidently, there are many exquisite buildings created by very talented designers, for example Villa of Water by Kengo Kuma Shizoka, Japan; John Lautner's Beyer House, and the organic fantasy by Antti Lovag near Cannes. However, many of the houses are simply good designs which appear to have been executed without a restrictive budget.

Hotel Design, *by Otto Riewoldt, Laurence King Publishing (London), 1998, 240pp, colour ills, £45.00*

In the last five years there has been a remarkable evolution in the design of hotels around the world. The avant-garde design movement of the mid-80s has now reached mainstream hotel chains, which have turned away from the characterless functionalism that had previously been dominant. The result has been the re-birth of individuality in hotels and a re-assertion of their role as attractive focal points for social activities.

This book provides a comparative and detailed exploration of 50 hotels, conveying to the reader a considerable degree of excitement – enough to enthuse even the most weary traveller.

Many of the hotels featured are spectacular examples which well deserve the attention this volume bestows upon them. The Point Hotel in Edinburgh, for example (by Andrew Doolan) is characterised by a highly stimulating use of space and colour and innovative design. Likewise, Philippe Starck's incredible flair for hotel design is represented by the wonderful Mondrian in LA and Delano in Miami, and the work of Barto and Barto by the impressive Hotel La Perouse, in Nantes.

Whilst the book is bursting with talented hotel design, some of the interiors featured do not possess quite the same appeal or design flair. However, this could be seen as a positive aspect of the book, since those who use this volume as a source of inspiration will hopefully learn from the design faults of less satisfactory inclusions, in addition to what can be gleaned from the large proportion of constructive examples.

The introductory text and individual hotel presentations are well-informed and very readable. The book concludes with a comprehensive resumé of each hotel that has been featured, information on the facilities offered, and details of how to contact them. *Hotel Design* will not only be of extensive use to hoteliers, clients and travellers, but should serve as a good source of inspiration for architects and interior designers.

DES-RES ARCHITECTURE

MATTHEW PRIESTMAN ARCHITECTS/PHILLIP TEFFT, MEWS HOUSE, LONDON

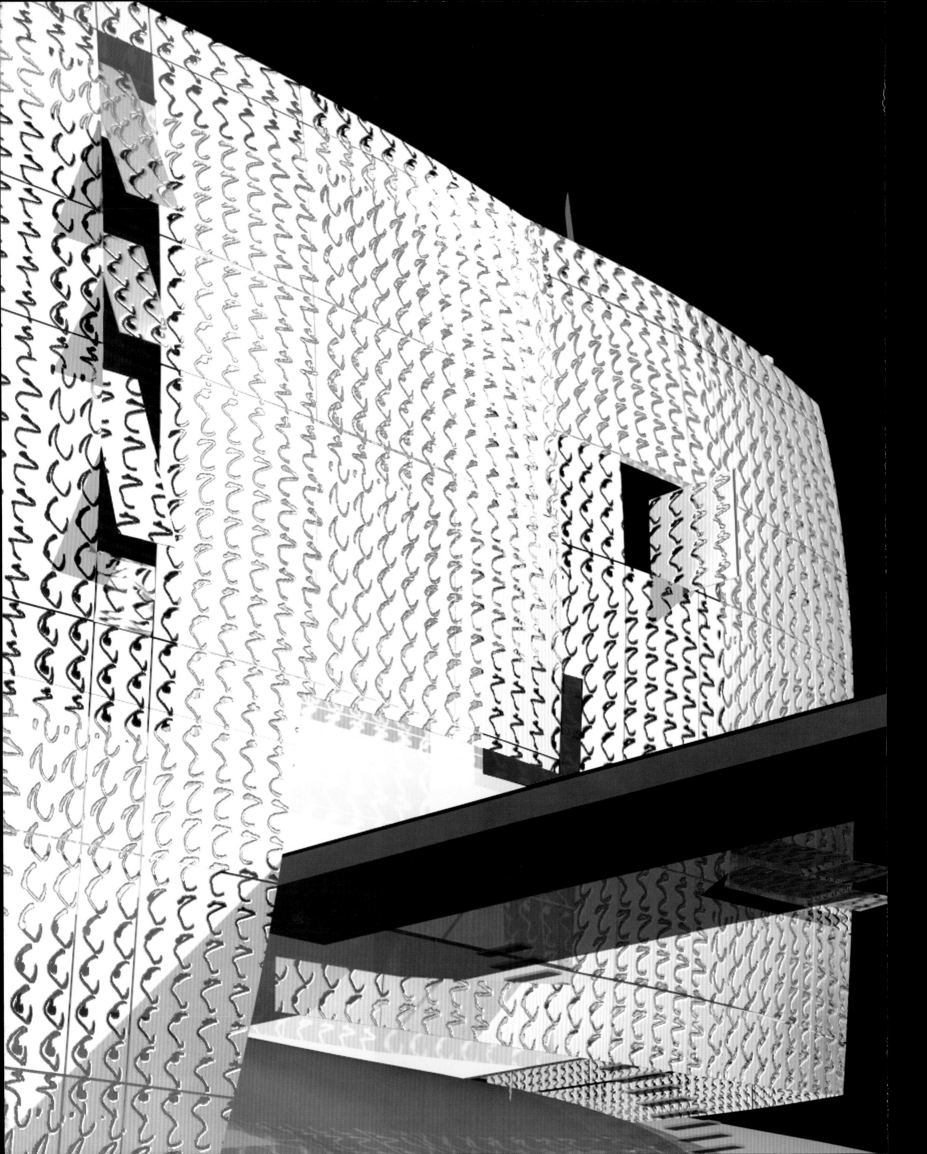

Architectural Design

DES-RES ARCHITECTURE

ACADEMY EDITIONS • LONDON

Acknowledgements

We would like to express our gratitude to all the contributors to *Architectural Design*.

All material is courtesy of the authors and architects unless otherwise stated. Attempts have been made to locate the sources of all images to obtain full reproduction rights, but in the very few cases where this process has failed to find the copyright holder, our apologies are offered. Photographic credits: *pp1, 92-95* Peter Aprahamian; *pp14-17* Abbadie Herve/Stephane Couturier; *pp20-23, 42, 44-45* Paul Warchol; *p24* Alberto Campo Baeza Studio; *p26* Warren McCutchen; *pp28-29* Tiggi Ruthven; *pp30-31* John Edward Linden/Arcaid; *pp34-37* Lawrence Scarpa/Gene Leedy; *p38-41, 66-69* ARC Survey Photographic; *pp46-51* Guomundur Ingolfsson; *pp60-65* Luuk Geertsen/estudi EMB; *p70* Michael Moran; *pp72-73* Kolatan/ MacDonald Studio; *pp78-81* Robert Oshatz; *pp82-83* Richard Bryant/Arcaid; *pp84-87* Chance de Silva/Dennis Gilbert/Frank Watson; *pp88-91*, Margherita Spiluttini.

Front and Back Cover: Ben Nicholson, Loaf House
Inside Covers: Eichinger Oder Knechtl, Monocoque, Schretter Apartment, Vienna, computer-generated image
Pages 2-3: Decoi Architects (with Objectile), Pallas House

EDITOR: Maggie Toy
DEPUTY EDITOR: Ellie Duffy
EDITORIAL ASSISTANT: Bob Fear
COPY EDITOR: Melissa Larner
DESIGN: Mario Bettella and Andrea Bettella/Artmedia

First published in Great Britain in 1999 by *Architectural Design*
42 LEINSTER GARDENS, LONDON W2 3AN

A division of John Wiley & Sons
Baffins Lane, Chichester, West Sussex PO19 1UD

ISBN: 0-471-98617-8

The Publishers and Editor do not hold themselves responsible for the opinions expressed by the writers of articles or letters in this magazine
Copyright of articles and illustrations may belong to individual writers or artists
Architectural Design Profile 137 is published as part of
Architectural Design Vol 69 1-2/1999
Architectural Design Magazine is published six times a year and is available by subscription

Printed and bound in Italy

Contents

ARCHITECTURAL DESIGN PROFILE No 137
DES-RES ARCHITECTURE

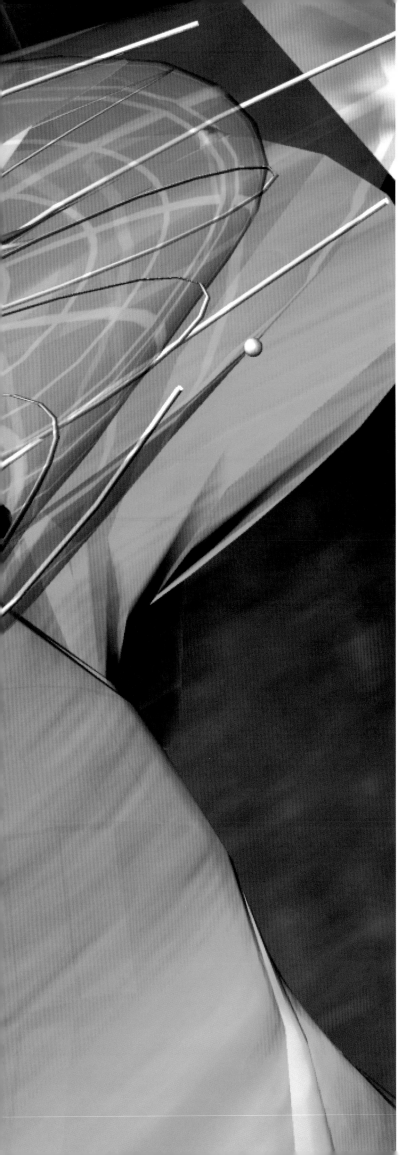

EDITORIAL
MAGGIE TOY

The advances in architectural design currently being explored by many architects are having little or no effect on the housing market. In fact, it can be seen from the results of recent surveys in the UK that the architect's involvement in the house-design process is usually considered to be distinctly disadvantageous in terms of the domestic property's value (estate agents are apparently no longer using the phrase 'architect designed' for fear that it will deter potential purchasers). And yet their years of training perfectly equip architects to design any kind of building, and in certain education establishments homes are given a particular emphasis.

The key players in the housing market – developers, builders and house owners – are generally unaware of, and perhaps unreceptive to, the recent developments in architecture that are intended to improve the built environment. For financial reasons, most homes are built *en masse* and on estates, and the majority of building speculators do not even hire architects to develop the designs, choosing instead to use old house plans that have been employed repeatedly throughout the country. Many of these were developed on the basis of cultural factors that may have been relevant for the way families lived decades ago but are no longer appropriate today. Developers, however, choose to use tried and tested plans and facades, not wishing to risk changes that might prove unpopular.

Many architects have argued that the average home owner complies with whatever the developer considers a safe option because they are offered very little choice. Perhaps lack of opportunity to dispel the mysticism of the architect from the mind of the general consumer could also be a factor. But the results of a recent survey, based on a mixed sample, commissioned by The Popular Housing Forum (PHF), reveal that while the public claim that they would like a modern home, when given the opportunity to choose their dream house it is almost always a traditional-style building. This fact is confirmed by the classicist Robert Adam, an active member of the PHF, who designs buildings that appear traditional and yet are suitable for a modern way of life. The aim of the PHF is to improve the quality of new housing. Their objective in the research is to discover and understand the factors that affect current and future buyers and to examine public attitudes to the appearance and site layout of

LEFT: Stephen Perrella with Rebecca Carpenter, The Möbius House Study, 1998

new housing. Many architects would not be receptive to this type of report and yet those who intend to pursue house design should at least assess the situation for themselves.

Whilst architects are frequently criticised for designing houses that are impossible to live in, when they design their own homes they generally stand by their principles – what better way to promote and explore your own ideals than to have yourself as a client! However, if public response was to be compared to two such homes, Crooked Pightle – the self-designed residence of Robert Adam, and the confidently Modernist home of Jonathan Ellis-Miller, it is likely that in a random survey Adam's house would receive more votes. There is, however, a resurgence of interest in the modern house project due to the fashionableness of minimalist interior decor, albeit a soft-edged version when interpreted for the popular market place.

However, the average person in the street is highly suspicious of the Modernist home. Therefore, if architects are to have any influence on the notion of dwelling in the next century, it is vital to get to the root of this attitude. This complex psychological issue is probably generated by recent historic developments that are linked inextricably with financial gain, and mass market perception of the value of traditional-style homes. The cool, slick lines appreciated by many architects are perhaps reminiscent of quick-build mass housing solutions of the 1960s to those who have not had the good fortune to compare the two.

Are architects designing on the whole for the limited audience of their own discipline? Should we accept that their influence will always be extremely restricted to those within a small field? The implications of the PHF report are that many of the homes that we as designers revere are not appreciated by a mass populus, and would not be sought-after by everyone. The work of Alberto Campo Beaza, for example, whose finely detailed houses convey images of peace, tranquillity and beauty would – according to the report – not be at the top of the general appeal table. A British television programme recently canvassed reaction to the astonishingly beautiful Modernism of Mark Guard, organising an Open House Weekend in his London house, and whilst most appreciated its aesthetics, they questioned their ability to live in it.

As a result of the structure of supporting finances, very few house owners are given the opportunity to dictate the design and layout of their own home, or to question how they would really like to live given complete freedom of choice. The new millennium and our increasing digital and computer literacy provide a superb opportunity to reassess exactly how we design our living environments and to question whether we should set aside old-fashioned, preconceived notions or whether these ideas remain relevant today.

The idea of Kit Homes has brought onto the market place the opportunity for middle-income clients to own homes from the designs of internationally acclaimed practitioners including Robert Stern, Michael Graves, Philippe Starck and, more recently, Nigel Coates. These can be purchased off the shelf and constructed by local architects or builders. Coates' Oyster House, built as a home of the Future in London's Ideal Home exhibition is an exciting step forward. Using a variety of new and sophisticated materials it provides a real option for those hunting for a modern way of living without an extravagant budget. However, these homes are not always what they may seem. Starck's Kit House mysteriously sank without trace soon after it was launched. And in a recent article in the New York Times, which had tried and tested several of the mail-order homes available in the USA, it was revealed that they all cost more to erect than was advertised and they can only be constructed by a skilled builder. Furthermore, whilst claiming to be highly original, many are mere variations on a traditional theme. Designs by less famous architects, on the other hand, offer a degree of individuality and may prove preferable when all the factors are assessed. Dennis Wedlick, for instance, provides textures and shapes; Sarah Susanka's design is simple and well considered and Duo Dickinson's residence has many details built in cement.

Geodesic dome house-construction companies are still thriving in the States, but while it is encouraging to see a new form in the housing stock, the designs are frequently modified and added to in order to mask the dome itself, thereby failing to realise the potential of the innovative design shape or the opportunity to reinvent the home situation.

In order for the way in which we think about our homes to change, new role models need to be created and we must continue to apply the developments made in architecture to the house. In their study for the Möbius House (featured in Architectural Design 133: Hypersurface Architecture), Stephen Perrella and Rebecca Carpenter have investigated contemporary domesticity in order to reconsider dwelling for the next millennium. The preliminary analysis revealed that the pervasive use of technology in the home presents an ontological dilemma. Current house formats are no longer tenable because space and time are being reconfigured by an informational geometry.

Perrella believes that dwelling has become problematic in

terms of Euclidean space as a result of media infiltrations – a force that implodes distance and replicates subjectivity as it enfolds viewer perception into an endless barrage of electronic images. Whereas homes were once conveived as ideal boundaries between interior and exterior, teletechnology contributes to a burrowing effect, turning the home into an exclusively interior condition. Perrella and Carpenter's solution for our future is the hypersurface, a transversal membrane that reconfigures binary notions of interior/exterior into a continuous, interwrapping median. It is difficult for most of us to make the transition between this type of research and the place in which we will be eating and sleeping in years to come, but it is exactly this type of groundbreaking experimentation that shoots us beyond accepted ideas and into the future.

Another aspect for consideration in the future building market, which naturally also affects the individual house market, is the use of advanced technology in materials. Developments in this area have not generally been transferred into architecture as successfully as they might have been, but with the advanced ideas of those pursuing hypersurface architecture, the development of these possibilities must catch up. Meanwhile, the clever use of a range of materials within design can assist both its beauty and its functional demands. Tanner Leddy Maytum Stacy utilise these factors well within their designs, particularly in their converted barn in Pennsylvania.

Apart from individual houses, there are of course many desirable residences within multiple housing schemes. Apartments in High Point – Lubetkin's North London residential tower block – are much sought after. And penthouse suites throughout the world command incredible sums of money. So if the idea of living in a purpose-built block is not universally objectionable, why is it that low-budget housing blocks are so singularly unappealing? Ernö Goldfinger's uncompromising and unusual Trellick Tower in west London may provide mass social housing but it is popular both with architects and its residents. The brutal style masks a well-composed living system that offers two-floor accommodation, a community-like street system and a magnificent view across London. But it is clearly an exception to the rule.

In his article in this publication, Francis Nordemann tackles the issue of mass, low-income housing ghettos. He explains how professionals who work on these projects struggle to conform to the massive restrictions under which they are working and in the end sacrifice their expertise by giving up a cultural definition of their discipline. He then goes on to analyse the vital requirements for community existence, whether in low- or high-income projects, and explores the issue of urban design. Many of the individual desirable residences featured in this publication are set within an existing, appealing urban environment. In mass development, on the other hand, the urban environment must be designed along with the architecture. In architecture schools the Modernist project frequently dictates that students should work on this form of housing and yet we are still not achieving successful solutions. Perhaps architects too readily believe the solution is in the built environment when other contributory factors to disadvantaged populations are the overriding influences.

In this issue, many aspects of the idea of house are discussed and we present a series of inspirational and desirable homes that demonstrate a range of possibilities of how we may live in the future. We can be sure that the question of our living environment needs to be reviewed and that many architects are taking on the task of interpreting our future needs.

Decoi Architects explore future possibilities for the home by using their knowledge of the concepts that have led to present formulas to project future directions. Their designs employ existing technologies and are therefore realisable in the foreseeable future. Many futuristic-type projects can be disappointing when built, losing something in the translation, but advance into the future must be strived for before it can be achieved. Studio Granda also ask what we should be aiming towards in terms of house design, both with their hypothetical project and their realised interpretations, which reveal skilful spatial organisation and elegant use of a variety of materials. The work of Sulan Kolatan and Bill MacDonald includes a complete reassessment of the nature of the house. They use their investigations into the urban environment to inform their interior structure, and the forms created respond to sites within a landscape. From these explorations fascinating spaces emerge and the resulting architecture is an exciting convergence of spaces and materials.

For Future Systems, the house of the future is already here. The practice combines a futuristic aesthetic with an ecologically aware construction that delights both owners and planners. The simple but sophisticated plan of their house in Pembrokeshire necessarily reflects the open, informal lifestyle of the clients, providing a home that truly reflects their living requirements. Characteristically, in the Laurie Mallet Residence – a conversion of an existing dwelling – SITE questions our preconceived ideas by using extracts and objects from the past. These are reduced to a ghost-like format that hints at what might have been.

HELEN CASTLE
REFLECTIONS ON THE OBJECT
The Modern House Revisited

When regarded exclusively as an object, the architect-designed house must stand alone, alienated from its domestic context. A coveted item, rather than a dwelling, it is aesthetically admired and pored over. It is photographed devoid of its occupants and the clutter of everyday life, exiled from people and therefore life in general. Thus it is cast into a mythical, unreal existence, with little or no reference to its daily use. This tendency to discuss and illustrate newly designed buildings as objects is identifiable as a distinct genre in current architectural writing and criticism, which, in Britain at least, has its genesis in Francis Reginald Steven Yorke's *The Modern House* of 1934. Though not the first book compiled as an anthology of houses, this is perhaps the most formative in a line of publications that has been dedicated solely to the modern house.[1] Like their prototype, most of these books are organised as anthologies of separate project descriptions, many of their authors acknowledging their debt to Yorke. In his *Key Buildings of the 20th Century* of 1985, two volumes of graphics and texts describing houses built between 1900 and 1989, David Dunster has stated: 'If there was a model for this volume, it is FRS Yorke's *The Modern House*'.[2] In 1995, John Welsh went a step further by creating a late-20th-century update of Yorke's tome, with the same title, bar the definite article.[3] A compendium of some 30 houses from the first five years of the 1990s, it cites *The Modern House* in the introduction as a touchstone by which to compare the development of the house since the 1930s.

Before examining Yorke's book more closely, it is important to establish the fact that there are many other ways of looking at houses. It is, in fact, the house's identification with people – architects, clients, owners, occupants – rather than its status as an object that has made it such an attractive area of enquiry for a whole array of disciplines. Most prominent among these are architectural, social, biographical and local history, and feminism. Not only is the house often interpreted as the self-expression of a specific 'artist', but, in a broader historical context, as a social container. Whether it is a large-scale country mansion or a speculatively built terrace, the house has much to communicate about a particular class in society at any given period.[4] For feminists the investigation of the domestic has been especially important: the emphasis on a 'woman's place in the home' and the cult of the domestic during the latter 19th and early 20th centuries has made the house an intrinsic part of women's history.[5] Conventionally, gender-power relations, like social relations, are most often shown through the spatial configuration of the plan, with its implied feminine and masculine zones, and through the oppositions of inside and outside (interior space being regarded as the woman's realm and the exterior space of the city, the street and work as the 'man's world'). In recent years, however, this approach has been revised and reinvigorated, the most innovative, exciting initiatives having been produced by Alice T Friedman and Beatriz Colomina. Friedman's main contribution lies in successfully overcoming the tendency of other social historians to over-invest in the plan. When investigating the layout or spatial configuration of a house, she examines its physical and experiential manifestation in the built work, as well as its graphic representation on paper. Colomina also departs from the conventional props of architectural investigation, such as the plan and drawings, by introducing a new tool: the photographic image. This, she has used in her interpretations of houses by Adolf Loos, Le Corbusier and Charles and Ray Eames.[6]

In print for more than 23 years, *The Modern House* reached its eighth edition in 1957. It first proved influential for a generation who, in the middle years of the 1930s, were hungry for modern architecture and for the opportunity to see the progress that had been made on the Continent. Maxwell Fry summed up its importance to himself and his contemporaries:

> We were all building houses for the brave sponsors of the movement, our first clients, and this book showed us where we stood, introduced us to architects as yet unknown to us, acted as an open sesame for a new type of Continental tour, but, above all, set standards of excellence by which we would measure ourselves, and examples that drew our affections and acted as a ferment for whatever talents God had given us.[7]

Successive generations of British students and architects who were limited by the restrictions on travel both during and after the war continued to look to Yorke as a reference for modern houses. As Reyner Banham wrote:

> The name of FRS Yorke is well known to my generation; a copy of his book *The Modern House*, bought in the middle of World War II, helped shape my own attitude to modern architecture permanently, and I am not alone in this.[8]

Given the place of *The Modern House* as a classic (Yorke himself recognised it as such in 1957 when he chose to add the first edition date to the introductory chapters rather than revise them), it is an unlikely combination of Modernist polemic, architectural specification and project description. Much of the main text is strongly derivative of Le Corbusier's *Vers une architecture* (1923), which was first translated into English by Frederick Etchells in 1927. Yorke is unswerving in his loyalty to the Swiss master, even when it forces him to tread a shaky, paradoxical line. Most of his introduction is devoted to overcoming the problem of having chosen to write a book on modern houses at a time when Le Corbusier had shown the apartment block to be the only acceptable unit for modern living in his utopian *Ville Contemporaine*. Yorke has to concede that the house remains an unsatisfactory, but necessary, form of habitation until other types of modern housing are built. This disclaimer is accompanied by his own

OPPOSITE: Ben Nicholson, Loaf House

Corbusian design of an ideal residential quarter with communal dining room and services.[9]

The photographs of boats, aeroplanes and ships in the first chapters of *The Modern House* share Le Corbusier's boyish enthusiasm for the new and the mechanical. An Imperial Airways Flying boat, for example, is labelled 'A modern product without precedent'. Le Corbusier's 'Five Points' – pilotis, free plan, free facade, long horizontal sliding window and roof garden – also reappear in Yorke's book in the chapters 'Plan', 'Wall and Window' and 'Roof'. It is in these sections, however, that the incongruent mixture of Corbusian-inspired polemic and technical specification becomes most apparent. In 'Wall and Window', Yorke's expounding of core Modernist tenets – the maximum use of glass and the construction of walls as skin rather than load-bearing structures – digresses into a discussion of the best products to create the most desirable wall surfaces. He particularly recommends 'Stic B' and 'Screetons Flat' as protective covering paints for concrete.[10]

The juxtaposition of the technical and the polemical in the book can be partly explained by Yorke's background and the specific period in which *The Modern House* was produced.[11] During the 1930s, Yorke (1906–62) belonged to a small group of mainly émigré architects, including Wells Coates, Berthold Lubetkin and Ove Arup, who advocated the adoption of continental Modernism in Britain. His involvement with the Modern Movement was such that when the MARS Group (the British wing of the CIAM) was formed in 1933, he became its Secretary. In the same year, he won a competition to design small, reinforced-concrete houses at Gidea Park, Essex, with William Holford, Gordon Stephenson and Alexander Adam. In 1933, Yorke also joined the editorial staff at *The Architect's Journal*. Two years later, he was appointed editor of *Specification*, which Maxwell Fry described as 'that remarkably concise compendium of practical information to which he remained faithful all his working life'.[12] Between 1936 and 1938, Yorke went into partnership with Marcel Breuer. In 1944, he joined forces with the Czech architect Eugene Rosenberg and Cyril Mardall from Finland, to form Yorke Rosenberg Mardall, now best known for their work on Gatwick Airport.

Taking into account Yorke's commitment to MARS in the mid-1930s, and his involvement with a tight-knit coterie of Modernist enthusiasts, the proselytising tone of *The Modern House* is easier to explain. At 28, Yorke was working within a milieu of young men who had just discovered the Master: Le Corbusier. In many ways, *The Modern House* is a tract, converting the reader not only to the Modernist cause but also providing an introduction, by example, to European work. Optimism for the architecture of the future was at its peak in 1934, the year of the book's publication. According to P Morton Shand of *The Architect's Journal*, 1934 opened 'fraught with magnificent opportunities'.[13] It was the first year in which Modernist British architects went beyond building individually commissioned houses, realising their designs for the first low-cost multiple-housing units. Projects included: Wells Coates' Isokan Flats, Tecton's Highpoint 1 and Maxwell Fry and Elizabeth Denby's Sasson House.[14] Modernism, it seemed, was about to fulfil its ambition to be a social as well as an aesthetic movement.

If the text of the opening chapters of *The Modern House* is grounded in Corbusian polemic and Modernist fervour, its other main elements – the project descriptions and the information on materials and construction – can be traced to well-established journalistic conventions. Their format resembles the sort of profile common in magazines for professional architects, including *The Architect's Journal*. Each description features exterior and interior shots and the odd drawing, whether plan or detail. The text concentrates on the technical elements of the houses, placed under such headings as: Construction, Walls, Roof, Heating, Windows, Doors, Floors, Finishes and Furniture. Once again, it exudes an enthusiast's zeal; this time for detail rather than dogma. The description of the roof of the Villa Stein/de Monzie by Le Corbusier, for instance, reads:

Hollow tile and reinforced concrete with 'Durumfix' waterproofing, gravel and sand. Concrete blocks cast in situ provide walking surface. Grass is sown in the joints to keep the roof moist.

Overall, this strange fusion of elements represents an extreme objectification of the house. To some extent this is due to Yorke's disciple-like following of Le Corbusier at the time. If his loyalty to the Master required him to abandon the individual house as the ideal housing type, he had to turn away from its analysis as a basic living unit for people, and present it instead as the architect's maquette on which to practice aesthetic techniques. The technical information, which is of the type compiled lovingly by the buff rather than rigorously by the technician, fetishises rather than elucidates the designs. As Dunster has pointed out regarding technical information:

Without proper constructional sections, much of it is ambiguous – and certainly does not clarify the problems of jointing materials together which led to those difficulties of weathering that gave 'white architecture' a bad name.[15]

Although Yorke's fixation on the house as object is explainable in terms of his own architectural and journalistic background, a broader explanation is needed to understand why *The Modern House* and other similar books have been so popular with an architectural readership. Why do books and articles produced for the architectural profession tend to preclude a fuller investigation of the subject while those written by and for those outside it seem to extend their focus to people and society? In her essay on the crisis in architectural practice, 'Losing it in Architecture: Object Lament', Catherine Ingraham succinctly describes the crux of the contradiction at the heart of the architectural process:

Architecture is not, contrary to its reputation, an object profession. Very few architects actually build, in a physical way, the buildings they design. It is a profession of object thinkers who grapple with the living condition of the object as a condition terminally other to itself. The carpenter or electrician – the trade person who actually carries out the instructions specified by the architect – is a different order of being from the architect, and this is testified to by the massive legal, cultural, and material conflict between these two worlds. What the architect has is 'knowledge of materials', and this knowledge is in perpetual negotiation with the actual material practices that the architect must marshal to his/her cause . . . the sense of object loss or object lament is a very long and deep strand in architectural history.[16]

The architect's obsession with the object is at its most fraught when he or she designs a house and not only attempts to lay claim to the object above those constructing it, but also above those intending to inhabit it. To appropriate the house as his/her own signatured work it is necessary to strip it of others' contributions, to emphasise his or her design and specifications. For the architect, the house is, in Yorke's words, 'the cheapest complete building unit for examination and experiment', rather than a house for living in.

Notes

1 The best-known late-19th-century publication of this type is Hermann Muthesius' *The English House*, 1908–11.

2 David Dunster, *Key Buildings of the 20th Century: Houses 1900–1944*, vol 1, The Architectural Press (London), 1985, p2.

3 John Welsh, *Modern House*, Phaidon Press (London), 1995.

4 Probably the most popular book to portray the house as social container is Mark Girouard's, *Life in the English Country House, A Social and Architectural History*, Yale University Press, (London) 1977. See also Stefan Muthesius, *The English Terraced House*, Yale University Press (London), 1984. Caroline Daker's, *Clouds: The Biography of a Country House*, Yale University Press (London), 1993, is an example of a book that portrays the house as both a social container and the product of its creator.

5 See Alice T Friedman's discussion of writings on the domestic realm in her introduction to *Women and the Making of the Modern House: A Social and Architectural History*, Abrams (New York), 1998, in both the main text, pp15–16, and in her footnotes, p30, note 19.

6 See Beatriz Colomina, 'The Split Wall: Domestic Voyeurism', *Sexuality and Space*, Princeton University Press, 1992; *Privacy and Publicity*, MIT Press, 1996; and for her description of the Eames House, 'Reflections on the Eames House', *Blueprint*, September 1998, pp41–45 (an excerpt from her book *Charles and Ray Eames*, published by Abrams, 1997).

7 Maxwell Fry, 'FRS Yorke, 1906–1962: A Memoir', *Architectural Review*, vol 132, October 1962, pp279–80.

8 Reyner Banham, *The Architecture of Yorke Rosenberg Mardall, 1944–72*, Lund Humphries (London), 1972, p1 of introduction.

9 FRS Yorke, *The Modern House*, 8th edition (1957), The Architectural Press (London), 1934, p3.

10 FRS Yorke, *The Modern House*, pp47–49.

11 For accounts of Yorke's life see obituaries: *The Journal of the Royal Institute of British Architects*, vol 69, no 8, August 1962, p303; and *The Architect's Journal*, 20 June 1962, p1371; as well as Maxwell Fry, 'FRS Yorke, 1906–1962: A Memoir'. Reyner Banham, *The Architecture of Yorke Rosenberg Mardall*, gives some details of later work after 1944.

12 Maxwell Fry, 'FRS Yorke, 1906-1962: A Memoir', p279.

13 P Morton Shand, 'Contemporary Trends', *The Architect's Journal*, 11 January 1934, p46, as quoted by Hélène Lipstadt in 'Polemic and Parody in the Battle for British Modernism', *AA Files*, January 1983, p71.

14 Lipstadt, 'Polemic and Parody in the Battle for British Modernism', p71.

15 David Dunster, *Key Buildings of the 20th Century*, p2.

16 Catherine Ingraham, 'Losing it in Architecture: Object Lament', Francesca Hughes (ed), *The Architect: Reconstructing Her Practice*, MIT Press (Cambridge, Mass), 1996, p155.

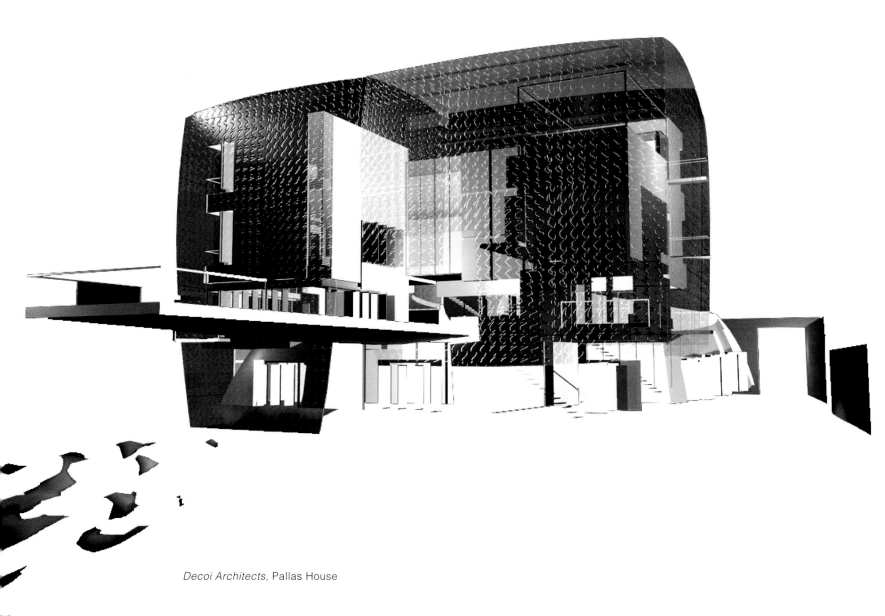

Decoi Architects, Pallas House

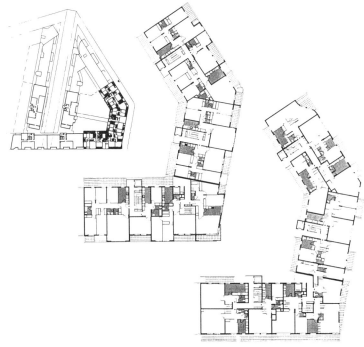

Bercy Corbineau, Paris, FROM ABOVE: Site plan; typical floor plans

FRANCIS NORDEMANN

FROM PRIORITY ZONES TO URBAN COMMUNITY
THE FUTURE OF 'LES 150 GRANDS ENSEMBLES'

During the post-war housing boom, millions of square feet of social housing, arranged in incomplete, isolated clumps, were tagged on to the outskirts of cities across Europe. Nowadays, these large residential districts, known as *grands ensembles* or 'big estates', are often run down. They have become problem-ridden zones, typically associated with the deterioration of urban life and social difficulty. Many countries continue to create such rational settlements, which cannot be thought of as truly urban. By exploring the past, we may be able to offer an urban future to these modern estates.

It is hard to believe – or to understand – what happened to social housing in the 20 years separating the construction of the low-cost housing estates of the Parisian belt, the Amsterdam southern extension, the garden cities of Britz in Berlin, or la Butte Rouge in Chatenay-Malabry, the Weissenhof in Stuttgart, and the Viennese Hofe, from the construction of standardised developments spread on the outskirts of large cities from Manchester to Barcelona, Amsterdam to Strasbourg, Lisbon to Frankfurt. It is tempting to see these projects in terms of a purely formal and stylistic analysis, which would ignore the structural causes of their problems, blaming them on the emergence of Modernism in architecture. It is also tempting to excuse them in the same rhetorical terms that were originally used to promote and justify them.

We might ask why, in the brief post-war boom, four million homes were mass-produced, stacked in towers and slabs on empty fields, far away from the existing urban fabric. Lying behind these projects are two myths – the myth of modern industry opposed to ancient, small-scale production, and the myth of hygiene opposed to the slum in the ancient city. The architecture of these estates was, in fact, a realistic, practical, even innovative, response to new complications that appeared after the war: the urgent need for the rapid construction of a large number of housing units, and the consequent demand for a greater number of low-cost dwellings (eventually produced *en masse* in imitation of industrial methods), plus the increasing desire to improve hygienic standards in housing. But in putting aside existing architectural, urban, historical and structural values, a new practice was also taking shape: normalisation.

Cultural values, which had long ruled the complex process of constructing urban settlements, were replaced by normalising and scientistic values that impoverished urban form. Projects were reduced to schematic compositions, forcing design to respond to the new constraint of standardisation. The era imagined a rational, urban world, its rules gleaned from modern industry; but when the patterns of industrial production were applied to the urban world, the results were almost militaristic.

In response to this shift of values, builders, architects and engineers struggled to conform, sacrificing their *savoir-faire* in the process by giving up a cultural definition of their discipline. Rejecting the complexities of urban design in favour of schematic composition culminated in the destruction of urban form.

The new process was made up of three steps: analysis of needs; listing of programme specifications and project. The project was no longer the whole process, but a sort of customisation, tagged on to the end and forced into the background. It was a pattern that could produce new objects: towers, slabs, detached houses, but could not create urban forms, even if it claimed to use urban models.

The impact of this process on the landscape can be simply described: high-rise towers and horizontal slabs dropped on the *tabula rasa* of public open spaces, which could have been parks and gardens. Dead-end roads and driveways instead of alleys, streets or avenues. Residual spaces at the front of apartment buildings that create a minimal relationship between inside and outside, instead of a planned sequence of entry spaces. Insignificant institutional buildings instead of civic monuments. In other words, with these projects, urban logic gave way to the random dropping of objects on sites.

Given the context of their production, it is hardly surprising that, 25 years later, these giant housing districts are in crisis: physically degraded and socially unable to develop into real communities. Their conception created the conditions of exclusion, precluding any possibility of integration within the urban fabric. They want to be recognised as a 'piece of city', but the planning methods that created them succeeded in pushing the city out beyond its own limits. The experiment never took urban roots, yet it is still in operation today.

Every town bears in a more or less implicit way the traces of urban historical models. Urban form stems from the cultural, economic and technical conditions of its development and, most importantly, it provides a meaningful framework that accepts multiple uses and transformations. In spite of their weaknesses, these housing districts are subject to the same rule; but, unlike other urban areas, their meaning cannot be found in terms of any architectural or urban value system developed over time (a model that would have taken root). Their composition signifies only the particular terms of their creation.

The estates' masterplan is terrifyingly simple, an exercise in elementary zoning for the novice planner. By failing to offer a public-space network with various relationships from outside to inside, it becomes a homogenous, formulaic composition, heralding an era of traffic networks (rather than continuous cities). These schemes are highly profitable for architects, planners and developers, creating an opportunity for contractors to hire cheap, unskilled workers to put together rough, pre-cast components.

Several million people live in these big estates, which reveal the backstage of so-called urban fabrication. Now that their weaknesses can be clearly identified, it is time to re-examine their original design in the light of what they could become.

A primary design weakness lies in their isolation from the rest of the city, the result both of their self-sufficient layouts, which establish a discontinuity with neighbouring areas, and by their particular form. A second major weakness is the simplistic treatment of architectural volumes and the poor quality of the spaces between buildings (or total absence thereof). A repetitive succession of basic horizontal or vertical blocks, placed as objects on the ground, is connected only by geometric figures (laid out in plan). There are no public spaces, continuous constructions or urban sequences. The same weakness can be noticed in the landscape itself, where instead of malls, parks, gardens or city squares we find huge tracts of empty and undefined land. A third problem lies in the heterogeneity of public buildings, social facilities and housing. Sometimes public services are concentrated away from housing (according to a theory of segregation), sometimes they are mixed in with it (resulting in a reduced density and increased dispersion of housing). In both cases there is rarely a clear physical or structural liaison between public buildings and residential ones; they don't seem to relate to the same city. The historical city is made up of a dialogue between solid and void. It is driven by the continuity of facades along a succession of public spaces. Estates, by contrast, are made up of buildings dropped discontinuously on undifferentiated empty space.

Finally, the organisation of a *grand ensemble* denies centrality: a typical plan consists of a linear artery, along which the housing blocks are distributed arbitrarily. The notion of a community, based on links between people and expressed by the continuity of urban fabrics, is missing. The idea of a town, formed from housing organised around community buildings, with public areas structured hierarchically, and therefore easily recognisable, is also absent. If an acceptable urban environment is to evolve, then the negative effects of such built-in standardisation must be gradually effaced.

Social problems like unemployment and poverty accumulate in such big estates because of displacement of social and cultural facilities, concentration of diverse ethnic and cultural minorities, disaffection of captive tenants. Images of slabs and towers are often invoked as symbols of the miserable living conditions of disadvantaged populations, the poor quality of the spaces being put forward too readily as a cause of misery. The production of such estates deliberately precluded their integration into the larger urban context, and the social and economic crisis also results from such exclusion.

It might be tempting to consider only these social and economic 'facts', and to advocate the destruction of these projects in order to eradicate the poverty they shelter (as if one could erase a historical mistake). But calling for their destruction denies the environment and history of millions of people. It is a call for exclusion and 'urban purification'. Disused buildings, or those in a poor state of repair, might warrant demolition, but it is unthinkable to raze structures to the ground if this action serves no purpose, if it does not pave the way for an alternative urban project.

Another option is to retain the original 'solution', promoting restoration to reverse degradation and neglect. This approach, however, denies the theories of urban evolution, and replays the logic applied to their conception: it supposes that, as with a machine, the problem of the large estates is one of maintenance and replacement of parts.

The first cultural step to be made towards integration is to accept that lessons can be learnt from these estates. The field is open to complement, densify, diversify the urban framework in order to enrich it, in the same way the ancient quarters were built.

The making of cities is a sedimentary process, fed and renewed by addition and substitution on a limited piece of land. Instead of extending suburbia indefinitely, it is time to look at empty sites as portions of 'cities-to-be', to develop their qualities and extend their history, to enclose them within urban culture and integrate an urban process – that of the traditional city together with its extensions. It is a necessary function of cultural renewal to adopt a positive attitude to these estates. The first step towards a more urban future is to confront and eliminate the logic applied to their conception.

Similar cultural problems were raised some years ago by the rehabilitation of historic districts. These were considered to be slums calling for eradication until attention was suddenly paid to historic preservation, immediately followed by urban investment. The modern estates, with their specific qualities, can be thought of as sharing equal status with other parts of the city.

Densification will call for diverse new uses and will bring cultural and financial investment. It will confirm that housing districts can be given urban value, can adapt to social changes and therefore acquire greater status. As long as studies reveal the positive aspects of modern urban frameworks, such statements can give direction and sense to ambitious, long-term political strategies aligned in carefully programmed and properly targeted projects.

Another positive aspect of these developments is that they are arranged to maximise the utilisation of sites and avoid waste of land (an economy underlined when compared to more recent peri-urban development). They also provide housing for many inhabitants. Huge, empty, misused and undefined spaces may be present between constructions, but these are potential sites. A varied socio-cultural community surfaces as a result of the original functional programming of the 'community' (a community = a neighbourhood = housing + services).

When a series of interventions is programmed over the long term, based on specific site studies, the housing district can be transformed, ensuring the conservation of local characteristics (such as lines of communication, boundaries, landforms, original architecture). Restitution of the local context and the specific geographic, urban and socio-economic characteristics and neighbouring physical and cultural environments would be a major step towards the integration of each social housing district into the city (and proof that the impersonal logic applied in their conception has finally been abandoned). Each case must be examined separately if individual problems of local restructuring are to be defined in detail.

Investment in public space can act as a catalyst in the re-evaluation of a community. Building into the empty spaces of large estates is an urban-addition process that enriches a site. Projects will make non-public spaces out of empty fields, offering sites for densification, creating new links towards continuity and achieving an improved quality of urban life.

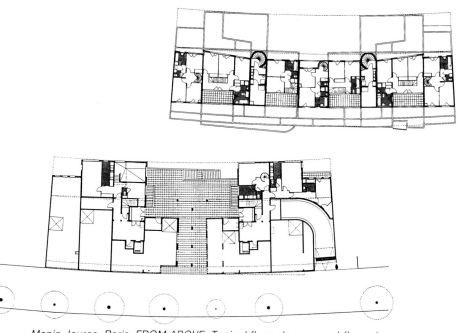

Manin Jaures, Paris, FROM ABOVE: Typical floor plan; ground-floor plan

FROM ABOVE: Glass Vessel axonometric; jANUS House sections and model

DECOI ARCHITECTS
THE INSCRUTABLE HOUSE

Poised between psychology and artefact, the house now carries an overload of conceptual focus that seems to implicate all architectural strategy. The concept of 'house', seen as the crucial interface between self and world, has come to be understood as an anxious form of contemporary identity.

If one can characterise the 20th century as an era of deconstructive tendency, of modern self-consciousness turning in on itself, then the house, as frame of that introspection, has been subjected to profound conceptual requalification. Thinkers such as Heidegger or Bachelard deplored the loss of memory and tactility of the modern house, stripped clean as a living machine, and blamed architects for the loss of habitability that it seemed to imply.[1] But from a contemporary perspective, now that the Villa Savoye or the Farnsworth House have aged to a point of almost melancholy nostalgia, it is evident that they have a resonant cultural patina (fossilised like the rubber Pirelli floor of the Maison de Verre) and have become deeply implicated in our cultural sensibility. The historic house, whose newly whitewashed surfaces are infiltrated by all the tubes of modernity, exists only as an ironic contemporary shell of 'originality'.[2]

Perhaps we can now recognise that the Modernist house, in its stark rejection of historic forms, highlights not simply a loss of memory and identity, but a shift in their cultural implication – a capacity, if not an appetite, for critical creativity and the 'shock of the new'. For behind Modernism lies a succession of powerful 19th-century thinkers who eagerly explored the apparently negative aspects of the aesthetically sanctioned sublime, celebrating the disturbing yet compelling opposite of all cultural 'positives'.

This surely prefaced the radical reworking of architectural form in the early 20th century,[3] and leads one to conclude that modern society is one of cultural trauma. This trauma was born of a vertiginous divorce from familiar patterns of memory. Whole new genres of memory, such as the 'originary memory' discussed by Freud in his celebrated account of the Wolfman,

were released.[4] As norms of cultural repression and privilege altered, new forms of cultural memory surfaced, nowhere more apparently than in the stark Modernist house: a thrilling historical voiding.

Evidently, other powerful influences contributed to this disturbance: the increasing transience inflicted on the modern worker by the wrench of industrialisation – exploded hyperbolically by the maelstrom of an entire world at war – uncoupled not only house from home, but illuminated the extent to which the *unheimlich* inhabited the *heimlich* in the dislocated modern psyche.[5] This is the insecure foundation that still constitutes the uncertain underpinning of the contemporary house and the psychology that attends it. We seem to have inherited a trauma of house that infiltrates well beyond its physical limit (if that limit has not itself dissipated and dispersed in public/private confusion). One responds by attempting to fill in the void (post-Modernist nostalgia for lost presence), or one chases after a disappearing referent with ever heightening deconstructive persistence, still haunted by Nietzsche's admonition that modern man is no longer an active creature, but a reactive one.

As we leave the 20th century, fully immersed in a post-industrial technical revolution and with a global consciousness (if not conscience), the anxious strategies of neo-avant-garde architects come to seem curiously historic in their reactive and self-conscious attitude. Witnessing such digression from the formulations of Modernist sensibility, one suspects that the house, or housing, is passing from the status of 'model' to 'norm'[6] – the norm being an indefinite and manipulable formula at the intersection of lines of production and desire, a much more supple and fluid fabrication than the finite model. Such a tendency, as if born of the fusion of technology and capital, seems to mark an effective dispersal of the Modernist architectural ego, and allows one to begin to imagine an alternative cultural tendency – a different psychology of 'house'.

Notes

1 Such outcry against Modernist architecture is amply covered in Anthony Vidler's suggestive book, *The Architecture of the Uncanny: Essays in the Modern Unhomely*, MIT Press (London), 1995

2 A compelling account of the 'conspiracy of white' and its authenticating mystique is given in Mark Wigley's *White Walls, Designer Dresses: the fashioning of modern architecture*, MIT Press (London), 1995

3 Here I depart from Vidler's argument, since I think that the line of 'uncanny' writers he traces might be seen as opposed to such simple nostalgia and the presentiment of a new cultural attitude – one of trauma, of a denial of evident memory – which perhaps came to fruition only latterly (in architecture) with Modernism.

4 Freud's shocking suggestion being that the most profound 'experience' of the

Wolfman's life was one that never actually occurred, but was fabricated in the imagination as trauma. I use this example only to suggest that the notion of memory was requalified in this period. One might suggest that there was a cultural memory-shift, with which we are still in the process of coming to terms.

5 Again, this is a reference to Vidler's account in *The Architecture of the Uncanny* of the sentiment that notions of habitation were radically changing, if not being entirely lost, in the development of the Modernist 'machine for living'.

6 This picks up on the argument of Bernard Cache in *Earth Moves: the Furnishing of Territories* (Writing Architecture Series, MIT Press (London) 1995), that we are passing from industrial to post-industrial norms. I extend this to the social domain since it seems to me that such logics have penetrated to the heart of the house.

SITE

THE LAURIE MALLET RESIDENCE
New York

The Mallet residence was designed in 1986 for a professional woman wishing to renovate and expand her 1820s three-storey, Greek Revival house, located in a historic landmark community in Greenwich Village. The dwelling had originally been developed as early speculative housing, and due to neglect, deterioration and its economy-driven construction methods, it required major architectural work. In fact, it was almost completely rebuilt, while still pre-serving the stylistic integrity of its historic origins. In order to expand the interior space, an innovative room was designed under the back garden (raised to accommodate this additional space) and the basement was converted into bedrooms.

The concept for the interior is based on a layering of narrative ideas, drawn from the history of the house, its context, and from the personal biography of the owner. This information was converted into a series of architectural features and furnishings that partially emerge from the walls, like the ghostly memories of several generations of inhabitants.

The choice of artefacts was determined by the scale and purpose of each room and by the existing architecture. A bookcase containing both real and cast volumes appears to emerge from another one in the adjoining house. A freestanding door-jamb marks the spot where a wall once stood. A phantom door implies access to something beyond the existing interior. Most of these objects are consistent with the life-style of the 1820s, although a few (like the equestrian references in the entrance hall) are based on the owner's personal history. A number of 19th-century objects, discovered during the excavation under the garden, were also used.

This work of narrative architecture is completed by a casually intergrated layer of Mallet's own furniture and artefacts. The result is that every part of the interior and garden has been invested with historical and psychological cross-referencing.

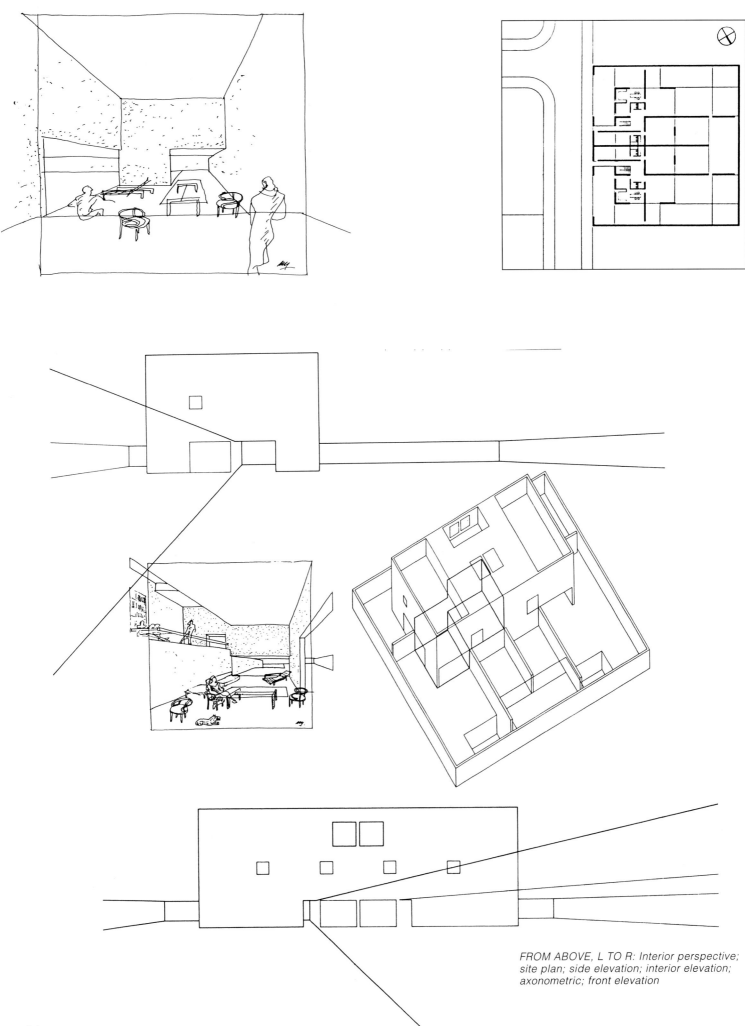

FROM ABOVE, L TO R: Interior perspective; site plan; side elevation; interior elevation; axonometric; front elevation

ALBERTO CAMPO BAEZA

JANUS HOUSE

Reggio Emilia, Italy

This house developed in 1992 in response to an international competition organised in Italy: *la Casa più bella del Mondo* (the most beautiful house in the world).

The requirements of the programme were resolved in a singular volume in which the space on the ground floor opens to a walled garden. The aim was to achieve a diagonal space, accentuated by a directional light. The main living room, therefore, diagonally connects two double-height spaces, which have the same dimensions in both plan and section. The principal source of light is a large skylight that opens to the farthest reaches of the ceiling.

FROM ABOVE, L TO R: Ground-floor plan; first-floor plan; cross section; longitudinal section; perspective view

ALBERTO CAMPO BAEZA

GARCIA MARCOS HOUSE
Valdemoro, Madrid

This single-family house in a conventional suburb on the outskirts of Valdemoro, Madrid, is sited on a 15 x 21 metre corner plot with two street facades.

The site is enclosed by ceramic brick walls, like a box open to the sky. In the centre, complying with set-back requirements, is a white prism with a rectangular base of 8 x 14 metres, divided transversally into three parts. The ceiling of the central, double-height sitting room is perforated by a long, horizontal skylight near the interior wall, through which light is admitted vertically. A large window, piercing the exterior wall at its lowest part, extends from side to side, echoing the horizontal plane. The resulting diagonal light creates a tension within the space.

Two other rooms are articulated around the central area. The stairs, kitchen and bathrooms are also situated on both sides of the main axis. The floors are of under-heated limestone and the flat roof incorporates a washing area, drying place and solarium. A garage is situated in the basement.

Through careful exploitation of light and proportion, a small, closed house is converted into a grand, open living space where anything is possible: a miracle box.

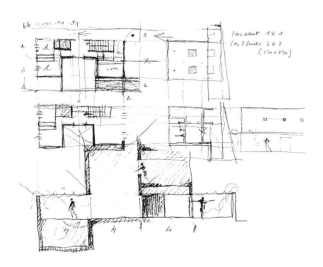

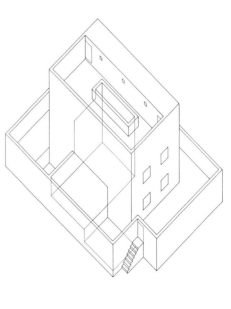

LEFT AND RIGHT: Sketch; axonometric

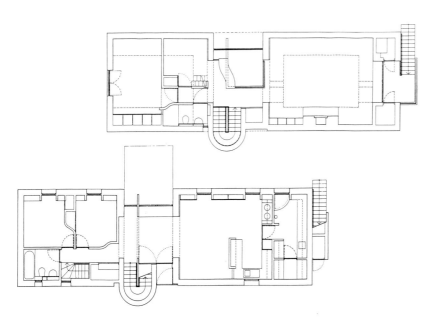

MARK GUARD ARCHITECTS
NEW HOUSE
Menlo, Galway

Completed in 1992, the house is situated four miles from Galway in a rural Irish setting overlooking Lough Corrib and the mountains of Connemara. Although adjacent to other new houses, the site is bordered on the west side only by mature trees, shrubs and agricultural land.

The clients shared our affection for traditional, rural Irish buildings. The desire was that the form of the house should be rooted in its historical context. These cultural values would inform design decisions and lead to an appropriate contemporary solution.

Unusually, the children's bedrooms are located on the ground floor, connected to a basement playroom and leading directly to the garden. The master bedroom, guest bedroom and living room are on the first floor, to take advantage of natural light, high ceilings and the view. An external staircase on the west gable, reminiscent of traditional barn buildings, connects the living-room terrace to the garden.

The interior is simply detailed and painted white. Sliding walls allow the house to be largely open-plan or divided off into more specific rooms as required. The guest bedroom converts to a study when opened up to the double-height hall.

The simple rectangular form of the house stands proud in the tradition of the Irish farmhouse. Seen locally as a radical, yet friendly variation on a familiar theme, the house is at home in the rural Irish landscape.

OPPOSITE, FROM ABOVE: First-floor plan; ground-floor plan; FROM LEFT: Axonometric; site plan

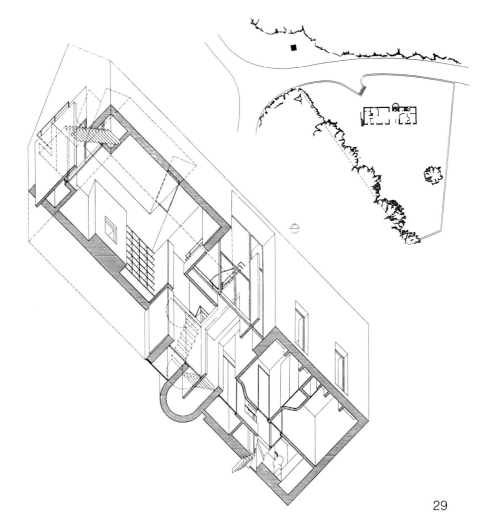

MARK GUARD ARCHITECTS
7/8 MARY ANN GARDENS
Deptford, London

The car-repair workshop purchased by the clients consisted of a two-storey, brick coach house, with garage space either side, under rudimentary roofing. The potential existed to convert the coach house into a two-bedroom residence, and by removing the roofs, to provide an entrance courtyard on one side and a secluded walled garden on the other.

The intention was to explore the possibilities of a two-storey garden with vistas and views on each level within the existing walls, so that the living room could connect to a roof terrace above an external studio.

The living room and kitchen are on the first floor and the bedrooms on the ground floor, opening on to the private walled garden. Windows on the west side of the coach house facing the entrance courtyard were bricked up so that the living space is not overlooked. The first-floor, east side of the coach house originally had no windows on to the view towards St Paul's church by Nicholas Hawksmoor, and of Greenwich in the distance. The entire east wall of the coach house was therefore removed, to be replaced by double-glazed sliding glass doors. Both on the ground and first-floor level, these can be slid to one side to open up the entire internal space to the garden. The separate studio

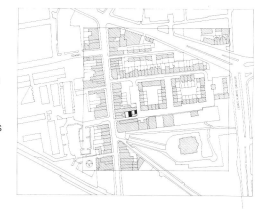

building can also become part of the garden by way of glass doors, further blurring the distinction between inside and outside.

The garden, an outdoor room, becomes an extension of the internal living space, and the generator of the design. Free-standing concrete walls define the spaces within the garden and support the sliding windows and the steel beams that brace the existing walls.

An entrance axis links the courtyard through the house and into the walled garden. This is reinforced by a linear pond and a new door in the walled garden, which terminates the axis and can be used as a separate entrance for the garden studio. It is intended that at the first-floor level a bridge will connect the dining area to the roof terrace in the garden. A small, double-height void in the entrance hall, spanned by a glass bench, draws attention upwards to the main space.

Floors at ground level are raw concrete, a smooth version of the gravel in the garden. Internal walls are white plaster, and details are suppressed. The kitchen makes use of stainless steel. All doors, both internal and external, including external shutters, are sliding.

The project was completed in Spring 1996 at a cost of about £80,000.

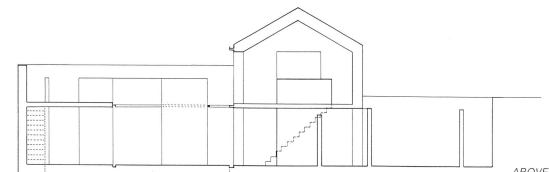

ABOVE: Site plan; LEFT: Section

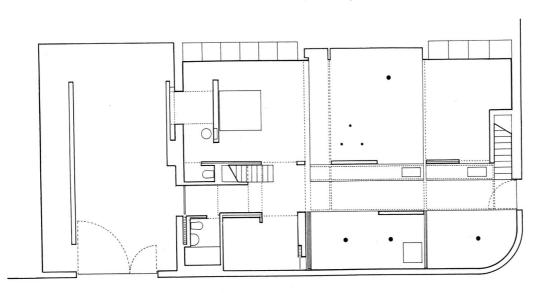

Ground floor plan

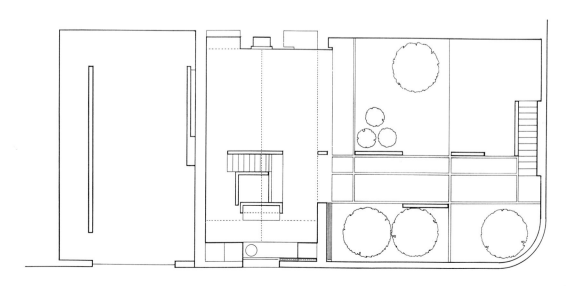

First floor plan

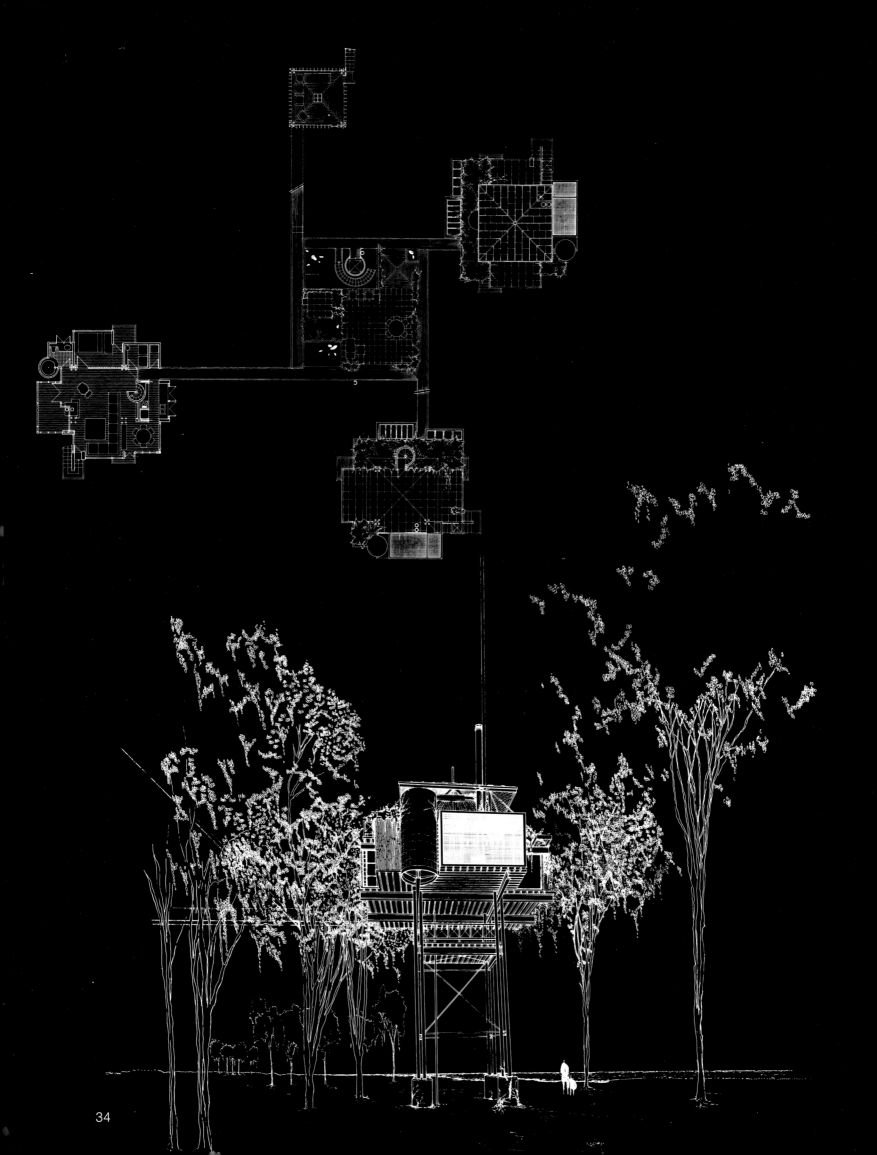

PUGH + SCARPA

TREE HOUSE PROJECT

Lakeland, Florida

The location was the principal inspiration for these four one-bedroom winter homes, each designed for the members of a single family. Adjacent to a lake in a Florida swamp with year-round standing water, the houses are surrounded by mature cypress trees and accessible only by foot on a raised, unpaved path.

Inspired by the Florida Cracker House, both in terms of imagery and energy efficiency, each structure respects the site's environmental fragility and is lifted 7.3 to 9.7 metres above ground level, into and sometimes above the treetops. The steel structures only imprint the site at four points, marking man's intrusion on

the site, while the remaining ground plane is organic and unaltered.

Beams and columns are of steel, pile foundations of concrete, and walls and ceilings of timber frame. Other elements include exposed steel, cedar siding, exposed timber beams, and galvanised-metal siding and roof.

OPPOSITE: Plan; sketch; BELOW: Site plan

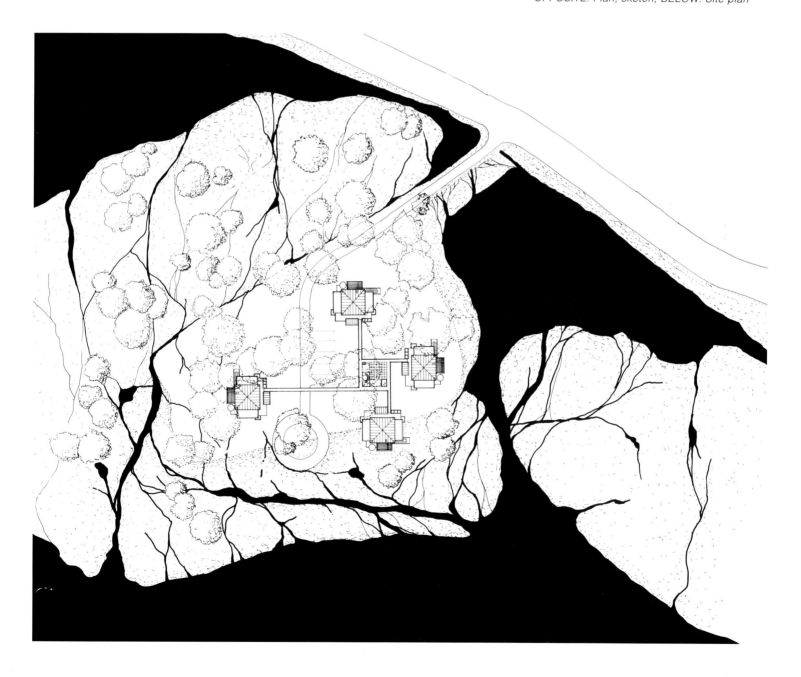

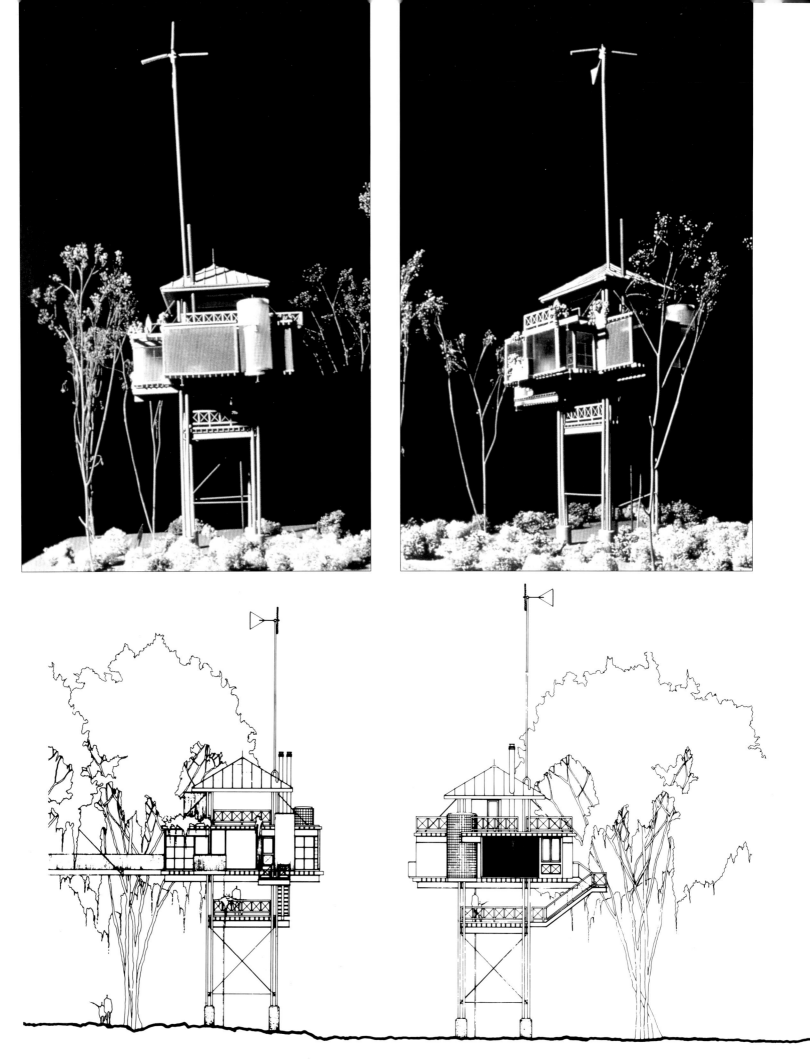

Partial site section showing building elevations and section

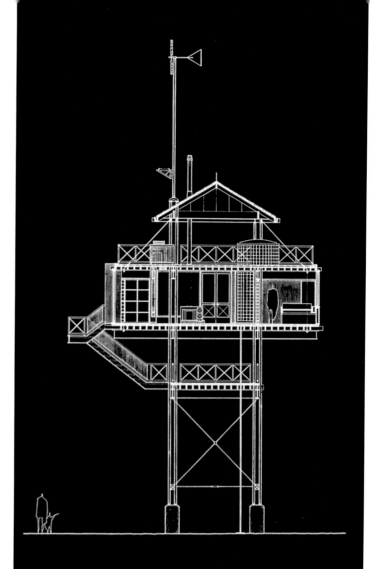

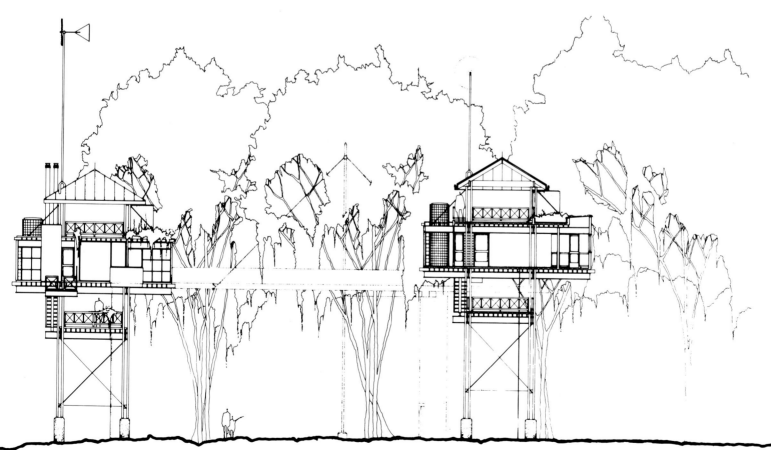

CLAUDIO SILVESTRIN
RIVERSIDE ONE APARTMENT
London

Claudio Silvestrin and Adam and Carolyn Barker-Mill first met on the south bank of the river Arno in Florence at the opening of the Victoria Miro gallery, designed by Silvestrin for contemporary art amidst the Renaissance splendour of the city.

In the summer of 1991, the Barker-Mills acquired a 232-metre-square apartment in Battersea, also overlooking a river, this time in London on the south bank of the Thames, between Albert and Battersea bridges. Set within the glass-block building constructed by Sir Norman Foster in the late 1980s, it offered panoramic views of the city, but very little else. In November, they wrote Silvestrin a note:

> We have been discussing the idea of redesigning the interior of our flat at Riverside One and we were wondering if you would like to create a Silvestrin masterpiece.

So Silvestrin set about his task, creating, in 1993, a peaceful space despite the frustration of being unable to intervene in the existing structure, with its low ceilings and perimeter windows. His first step was to open up the north-south axis (flanked on one side by a long stretch of floating, solid-white wall), through which the cityscape projects uninterrupted from one end of the apartment to the other. Flowing across the entire space, large slabs of Tuscan *pietra serena* stone echo the calm grey ribbon of the Thames.

A floor-to-ceiling, curved, satin-glass screen separates the doorless kitchen and bedroom areas from the more public spaces of the living room and study, yet also reveals and unites the elements on either side through their shadows and silhouettes, cast against its surface. To the west, floor-to-ceiling, satin-glass

screens act both as barrier to, and enhancer of, the outside light. Solid and stretched interior wall expanses incorporate Adam Barker-Mill's light sculptures.

The geometric pieces of furniture are one-off designs by Silvestrin, as are the fixtures and fittings, from the flush lighting discs and elegant wooden tap fittings to the stone kitchen island, bathroom basins and pear-wood tables and benches.

Countless sophisticated details veil the technology, all the functions being concealed behind fully stretched glass screens, floor-to-ceiling cupboard doors and walls. This creates an air of silence and abstraction. The choice of natural materials is rigorous, their qualities coming alive to the senses due to the monolithic, pure forms through which they are presented.

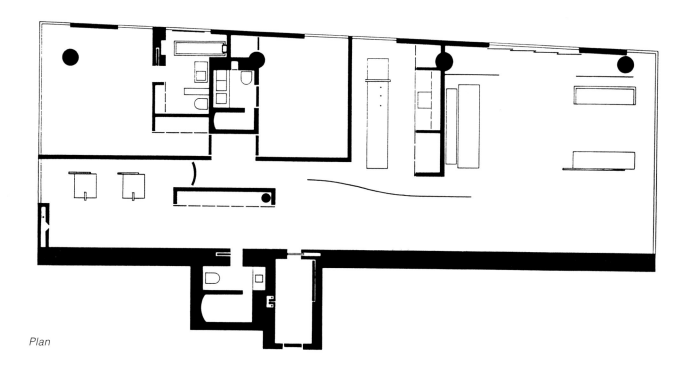

Plan

TANNER LEDDY MAYTUM STACY

PRIVATE RESIDENCE

Chester County, Pennsylvania

This project of 1993 creates a critical dialogue between old and new; a compression of past, present and future into a living history of place.

The clients wished to create a 325-metre-square, single-family home within an existing barn, in a manner both respectful of the original form, materials and volumes and expressive of its new use.

Located in south-eastern Pennsylvania, the barn was built in 1820 and consists of 50.8-centimetre-thick field-stone walls supporting hand-hewn oak timbers at floor and roof. The original exterior openings were minimal, including arched apertures at the first level, a large barn door, a smaller threshing door at the second level, and narrow ventilation slits, or 'wind-eyes', at the second level and above. The surrounding area, once agricultural in character, is now mainly residential.

Rather than mummify the past, this project creates a relationship between past and present. The new structure, a smooth, cherry-wood box, sits within the rough, stone shell. The inner, timber wall carries all structural loads and building systems, thus relieving the outer wall of pressure and exposing it at intervals in the interior. The space between old and new walls accommodates circulation, fireplaces and intimate seating areas near the light. As they move through this intermediate space, the inhabitants literally brush against the history of their place.

The simple dignity of the old structure has been respected. New openings have been kept to a minimum and existing materials retained. Original apertures at the first level are fitted with modern steel windows and doors. The 'wind-eyes' accommodate contemporary, operable windows. An opening in the east wall replaces the threshing door and faces on to a deck carved out of the existing porch roof. The main roof has been perforated with skylights to minimise new openings in the stone walls. A family of metal-clad forms, expressive of an abstracted agrarian vocabulary, arranges itself against the stone barn.

The simple palette of unadorned materials, assembled in a straightforward manner, is used in relation to the original materials to further develop the past/present dialogue. A new steel structure supports old, hand-hewn, oak beams. White maple stairways slide between rustic stone and smooth cherry plywood walls. An opening in the second floor exposes original oak-floor timbers and allows light to enter the floor below. A steel, glass and maple catwalk hovering above the existing oak roof structure connects master bedroom and dressing area across a 9-metre-high volume. On the first floor, Pennsylvania flagstone and bare concrete floors denote the outer and inner zones that recur throughout the house.

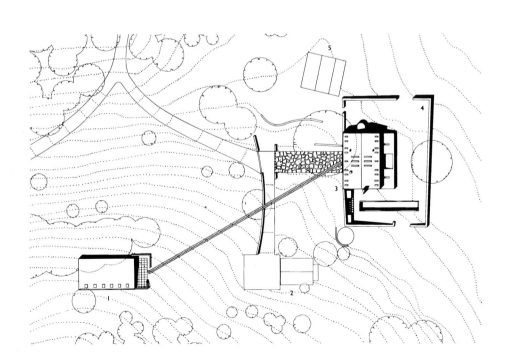

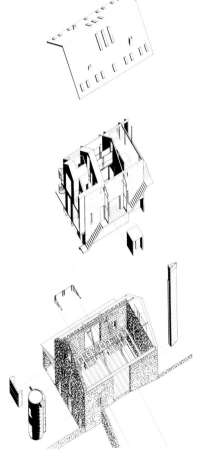

ABOVE: Site plan showing new painting studio (1), new garage in existing corn crib (2), new dwelling in existing barn (3), existing paddock (4), existing house (5); RIGHT: Exploded axonometric

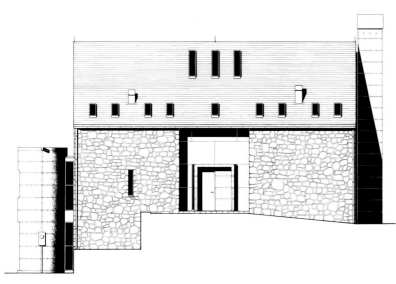

LEFT TO RIGHT: Elevation; second-level plan

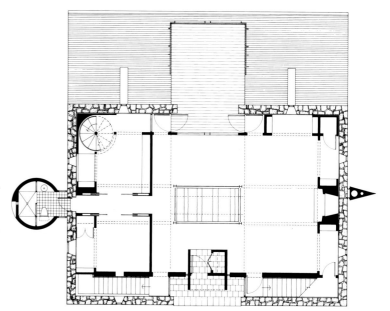

44

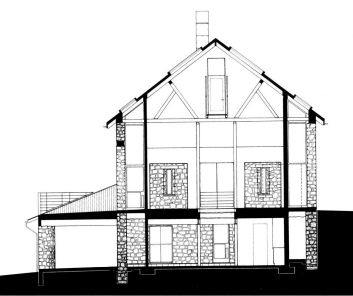

LEFT TO RIGHT: Section; third-level plan

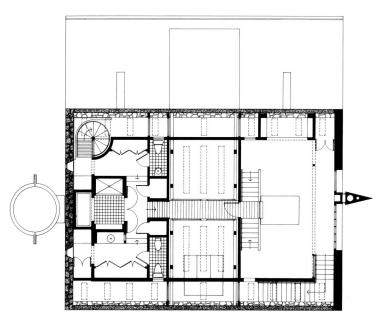

STUDIO GRANDA
HOUSE OF 19

This conceptual work was designed in 1994 for Icelandic artist, Thorvaldur Thorsteinsson and his family. Regular meetings were held between the artist and the designers, in which a framework for the project was formed. This became the basis for the client's list of 19 requirements:

1 Large kitchen close to living room – big table
2 Bright bedroom close to bathroom
3 Spare bedroom (for teenager)
4 Large bathroom with shower only – heated floor
5 50-metre^2 workroom with large work table, sofa and one clean wall
6 Lots of bookshelves except in bedroom
7 Small bookshelf in toilet
8 Bathrooms close to workroom, bedrooms and kitchen
9 Stairs up and stairs down
10 Possibility to sit and work in different directions
11 Minimum of two dissimilar places to sit with guests
12 Possibility to open/walk-out from kitchen, workroom and bedroom
13 Easy disposal of waste – especially bottles and cans
14 Ironing board, mop, vacuum cleaner etc to hand but not in way
15 Large clothes cupboard close to bedroom
16 View to stars for gazing
17 Variable lighting to change ambience in rooms and distinguish between spaces
18 Music controlled remotely – connected to computer
19 No wooden floors – tiles and mats

The house is built with no specific location or site in mind. It can be likened to a data-disc containing essential information and elements of human reference for universal application. It contains all the necessary elements for living and for supporting the lifestyle of the family and is capable of insertion into any built or un-built fabric. As the artist has no desire to differentiate himself from the other people living in the vicinity, the external form of the house is indistinguishable from that of the adjacent buildings.

The visual relationship between the interior of the house and the immediate neighbourhood is of little consequence, for life outside the dwelling is viewed only through the technological window of television. But, aware of the filtered quality of the electronic media, the artist checks the stars daily to confirm his position, simultaneously taking precise climatic readings.

The members of the family perform various activities in a series of spaces distributed around a ramp. These areas can be further subdivided by padded curtains to provide the required acoustic, visual, mental or olfactory privacy. Natural light, which enters from the glazed core, may also be controlled by the curtains as it gradually changes during the daily and yearly cycle. Since generous provision for rest is essential for bodily health, the padded curtains can be removed from the rail and lounged on while watching television or thinking.

A house is the most private and personal of all buildings. Its design and what it contains expresses much about the nature and personality of its inhabitants. House of 19 communicates this through drawings, a model and the artist's writings about life within the house.

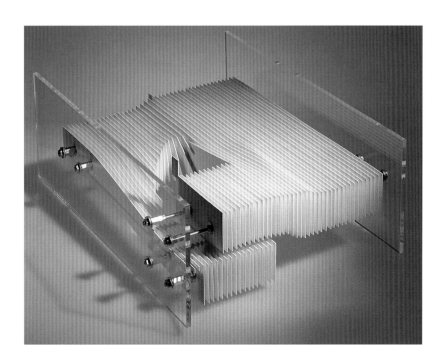

STUDIO GRANDA
ÁSENDI HOUSE
Reykjavík, Iceland

Constructed in 1996, this 80-metre-square extension to an early 1960s villa was built to accommodate bedrooms, a bathroom and a breakfast bar for the clients' two children. In addition there are work/storage areas.

The existing single-storey house was built on a restricted corner site. Its detached double garage was adopted as a storage and workroom. The new accommodation was placed above it, connected to the existing house via a new entrance hall. Above the hall, a sun terrace serves the breakfast bar of the children's wing.

The external fabric and form of the extension mimic that of the original house and endeavour to reduce the impact of modifications made during the 1980s. By introducing a second storey, the corner location is reinforced, a quality enhanced by the scale and proportion of the fenestration. New landscape works for the entrance and car-parking areas use primal material: hewn basalt, earthy paviors, *iroko* and granite setts. The same setts, sawn in slices, are employed in the entrance hall.

Above the main entrance is an artwork by Lilja Pálmadóttir, especially commissioned by the clients.

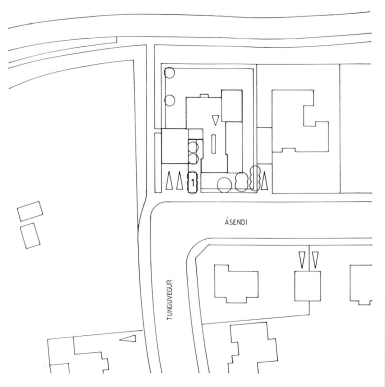

Site plan

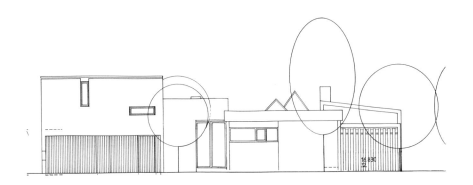

LEFT: West elevation; OPPOSITE, FROM ABOVE L TO R: Ground-floor plan; first-floor plan; north elevation; section

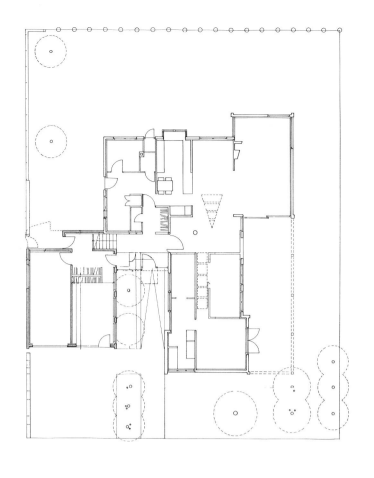

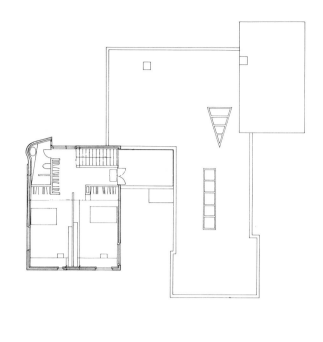

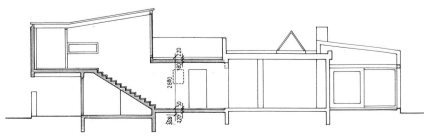

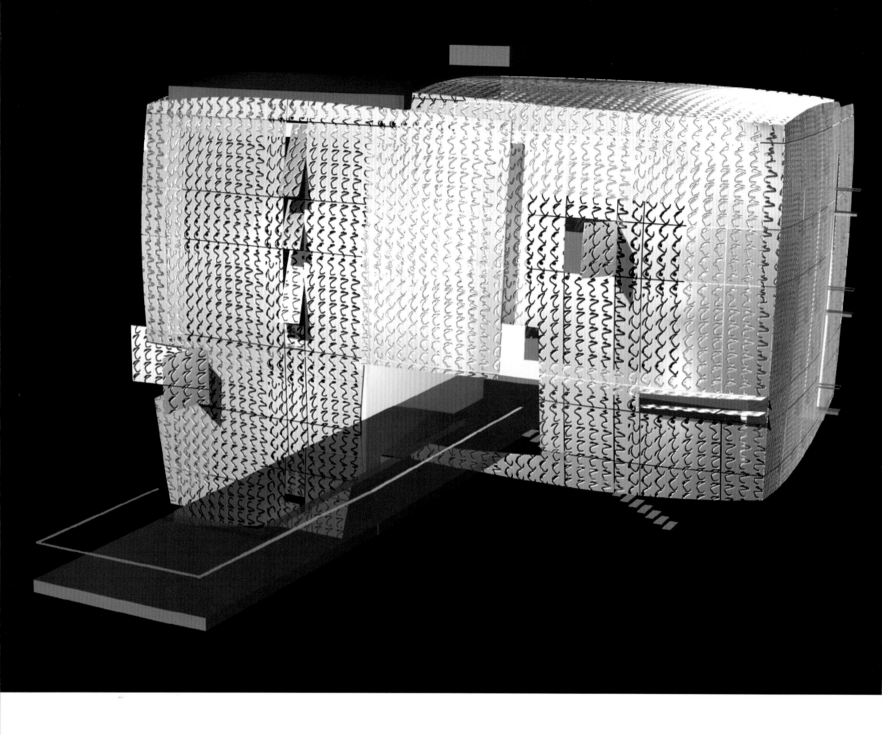

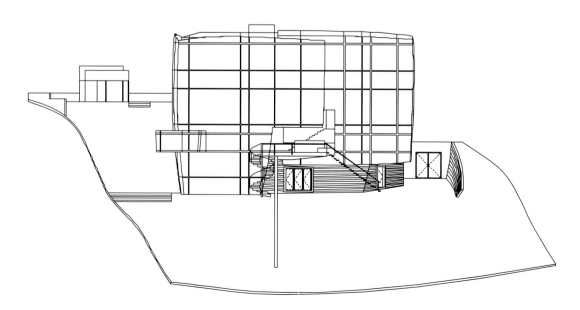

DECOI ARCHITECTS (WITH OBJECTILE)
PALLAS HOUSE

The Pallas House (1996) is a subtly amorphous form, whose embedded structure emerges from the ground as a restrained, mute shrouding, a curvilinear, metallic filter, which obscures the translucent house within. This 'light positive' – an arabesque carved delicately from the air – is held against the sculptural, languid forms of the landscape – a 'heavy negative' carved from the fluid earth.

One enters through a dark vortex, (the massive walls levitating sinuously), to a luminous void – a suspension of chiselled tracery that envelops the house, filtering the harsh environment.

The forms are at once simple and complex. A subtle deformation of surface is achieved through the use of sophisticated software. The warped stone walls of the landscape and the complex, curved shells of the carapace quietly distort the logics of industrial production to hint at a non-standard, post-industrial form. From the perforations of the metallic skin (trappings of movement), to the flutter and swell of the landscape, the project is generated numerically: chance-calculus imaginings of precise indeterminacy. Expressivity seems to implode, both in the generative process and in the final form, which have in any case fused as process.

The metallic filter was fabricated directly by numeric command machine, the linkage of creative machine and manufacturing machine opening up the field to non-standard complexity, to new numeric genres of decoration and organicism.

The Pallas House seems to be caught between logics, as if it were the reflection of a change-of-state, a mirror-image of representative collapse. The name Pallas refers to the twin sister murdered by the enigmatic and eidetic goddess, Helen. Here, the original sin at the root of all representative structure is exposed as the image becomes primary.[1]

Internally, the house is organised around a central void as a series of rectilinear boxes of translucent glass, which catch the patterns of light falling through the filtering screen and shroud the bodies moving within. These, too, seem to have undergone a formal glaciation, the cuts and abrasions in the crystalline surfaces quietly marking traces of slippage and movement, as if they were scars of emergence.

The spaces are translucent chambers of light-patterning (above), or voluptuous heavyweight wrappings (below) – forms of mute antithesis. But there is a sixth sense in the swelling shapes, as in the enigmatic calligraphy, of an imminent formal release, a potential for decorative excess. This rebirth of organic and decorative form within the interstices of a proliferating numeric capacity marks a new form of post-industrial profligacy.

Note

1 Working on the house with Bernard Cache, we were conscious of a profound shift in the manner of representation, whose temporal logics seem curiously suspended by CAD logic. The image is primary (a formulation from Cache's *Earth Moves: The Furnishing of Territories, Writing Architecture Series,* MIT Press (London), 1995) in the sense that it is a manipulable matrix of possibility, a form that at any moment is subject to change in response to any number of impinging criteria (client, budget, climatic data, etc). The image in no way re-presents something that is prior to it, but is the active generator of form. In this case we generated six different facade solutions in wood, metal, plastic, etc, perforated with morse code, calligraphic runes and electronic hieroglyphs.

OPPOSITE: Elevation; RIGHT, FROM ABOVE: Objectile prototype panel; motif

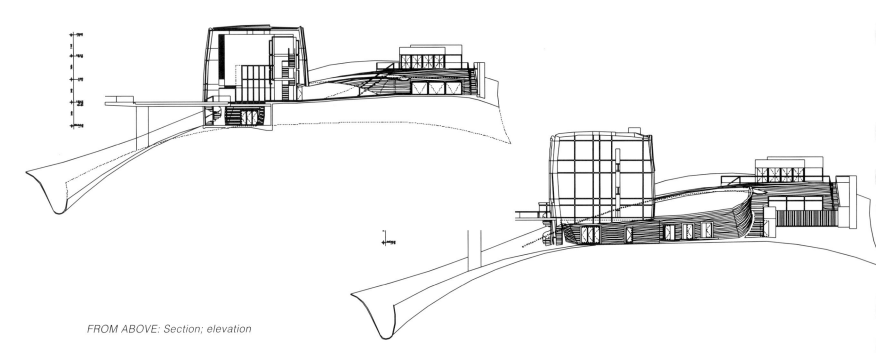

FROM ABOVE: Section; elevation

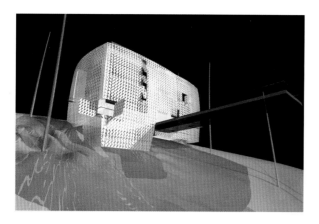

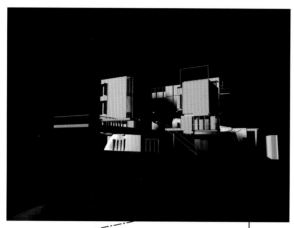

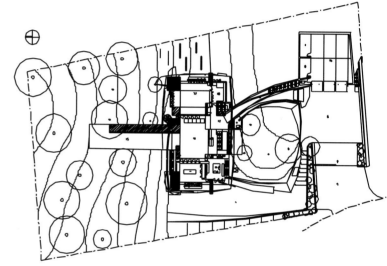

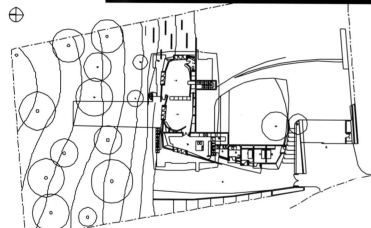

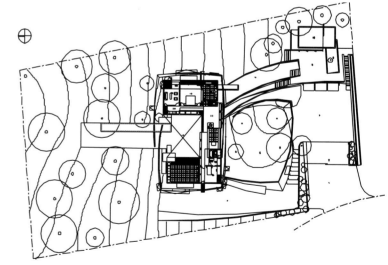

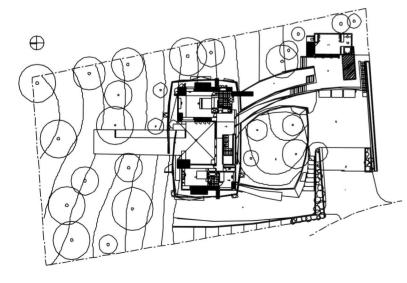

Plans

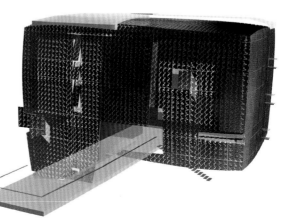

55

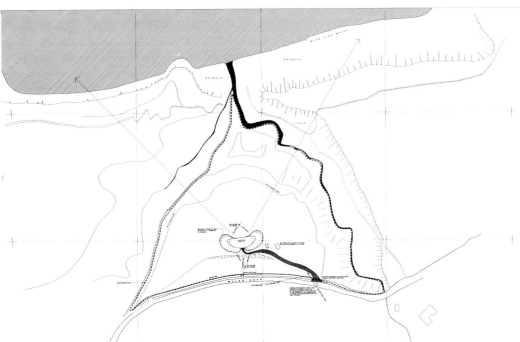

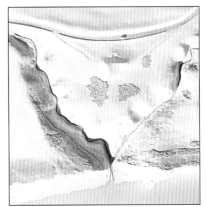

FROM ABOVE: Model view from the sea; site plan; aerial view, model

FUTURE SYSTEMS

PROJECT 222
Druidstone Haven, Wales

The beautiful and dramatic location of this house, set within the Pembrokeshire Coast National Park, was the driving force of the design. The objective of this project (1996) was both to maximise the stunning views of the Welsh coastline and to minimise the visual impact of the building by siting it in a way that makes it appear to be a natural part of the landscape.

The soft, organic form of the house is designed to melt into the rugged grass and gorse landscape, the roof and sides of the house being turfed with local vegetation. Views of the building are thus only of these grasses and the transparent glass walls outlined by a slim stainless-steel rim – an eye overlooking the sea. The surrounding landscape remains untouched, with no visible boundary lines or designated garden area, ensuring the building's organic appearance.

The simple plan is open and informal, reflecting the lifestyle of the clients, with the main seating area arranged around an open log fire. Two free-standing, brightly coloured, prefabricated pods house the bathroom and kitchen services without touching the roof, in order that the space is perceived as a totality. A continuous blockwork retaining wall and steel-ring beam support the roof, eliminating the need for internal columns.

The roof is an aerofoil construction covered with turf. Its curved plywood underbelly creates a soft interior, complementing the organic form of the structure. The house is entirely electrically powered, with under-floor heating elements arranged around the perimeter walls.

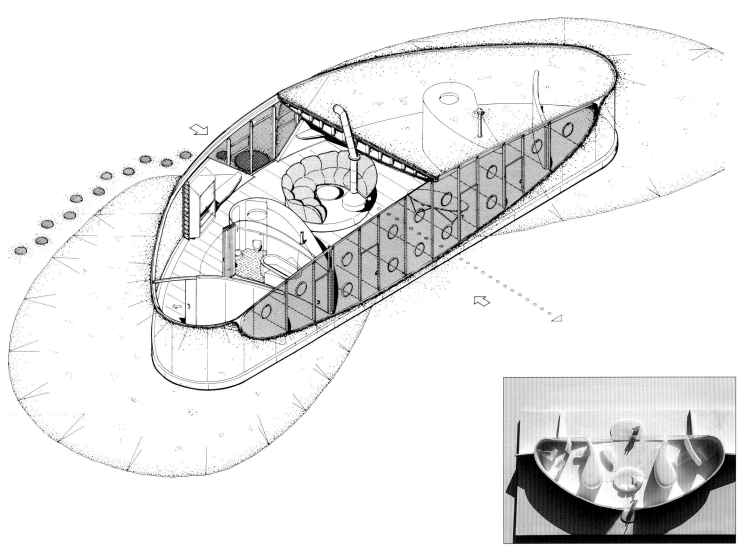

FROM ABOVE: Isometric; model

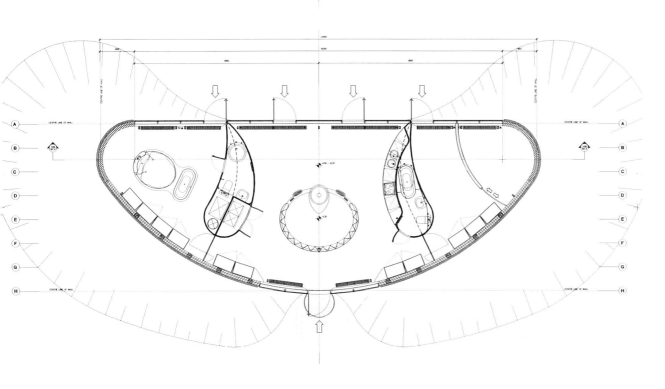

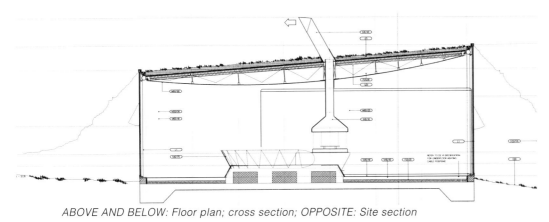

ABOVE AND BELOW: Floor plan; cross section; OPPOSITE: Site section

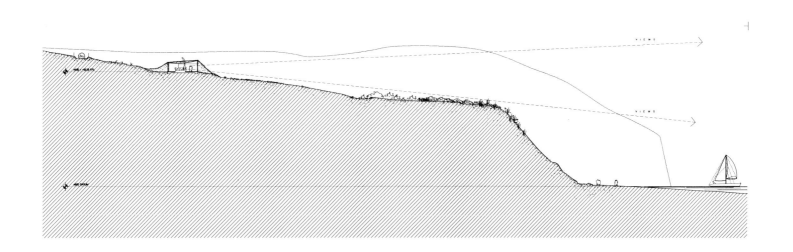

ENRIC MASSIP-BOSCH

CASA CABRILS
Barcelona

This renovation of a single-family detached house, completed in 1997, transforms the use, form, number and relationships of several existing spaces, enlarging the programme and redefining garden levels and points of access. The entrance is placed at the lowest level, along with a new underground garage. Garden terraces are altered in order to allow for a continuity between inside and out. A new pavilion by a swimming pool houses the living room.

An interior staircase and a fresh distribution of spaces remodulates the interior of the existing house. Unity between the original building (which had to be maintained due to regulations) and the new additions is achieved in the interior by means of the visual and physical communication of spaces, and externally through the use of a limited palette of colours, materials and textures, particularly the oxidised finish of walls and corten plates.

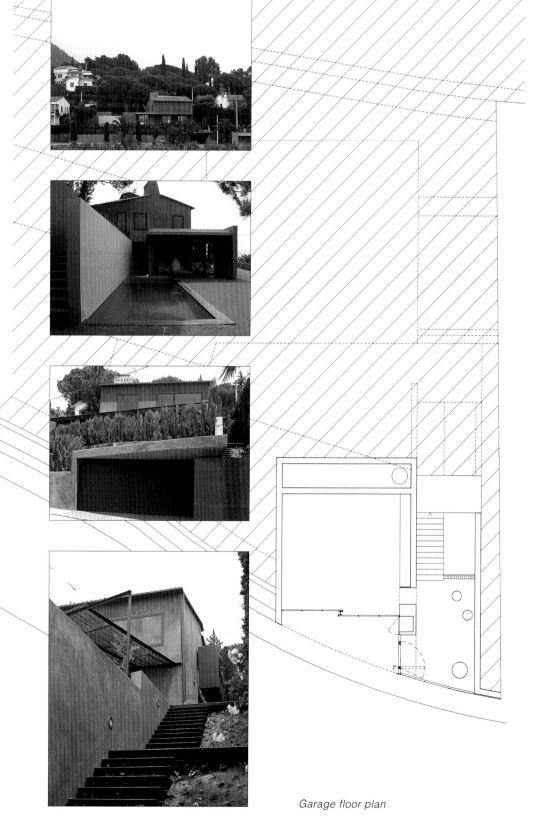

Garage floor plan

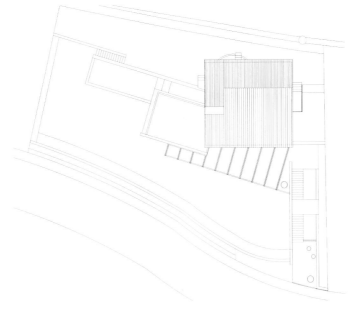

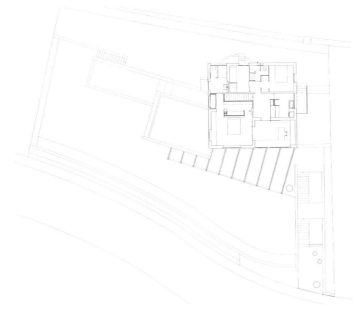

*FROM ABOVE: Roof plan;
second-floor plan; first-floor plan*

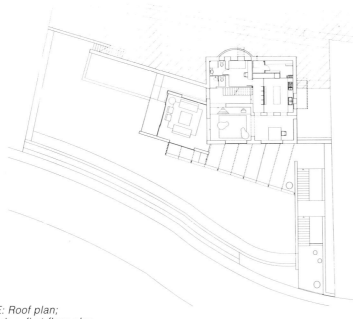

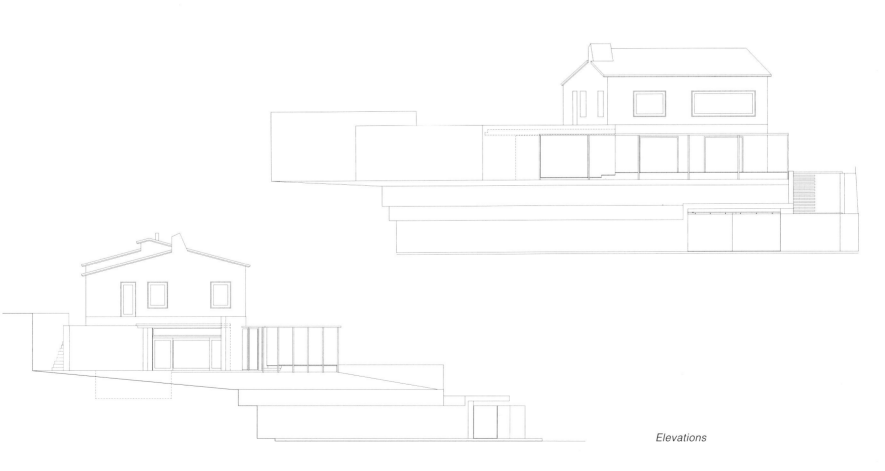

Elevations

DE BLACAM + MAEGHER

MEWS HOUSE

Heytesbury Lane, Dublin

The 18-square-metre house, completed in 1997, is located on a narrow mews plot, adjacent to a late-Georgian terrace with an east-west orientation.

The constraints of the site did not permit natural light. As a result, a top-lit, double-height atrium was introduced, which opens three sides of the house to natural light. It also creates an extra cedar-panelled facade, which wraps around to the entrance court.

The main living area on the ground floor connects the entrance court in the east to the garden in the west. The master bedroom has a dual aspect overlooking the atrium and opening onto a hardwood roof deck. Granite setts lead to the white limestone floor of the atrium and garden terrace, while the flooring of the living space is of oak.

BELOW: Axonometric

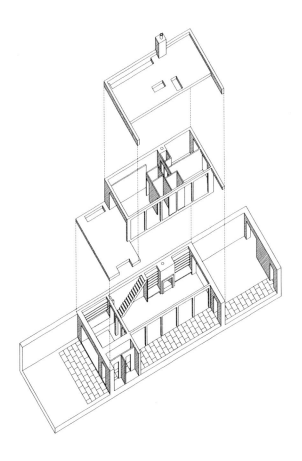

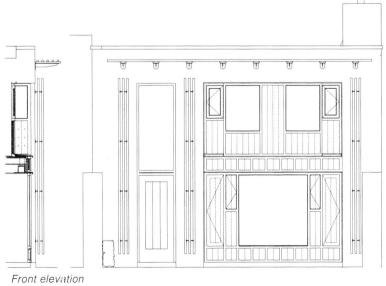

Front elevation

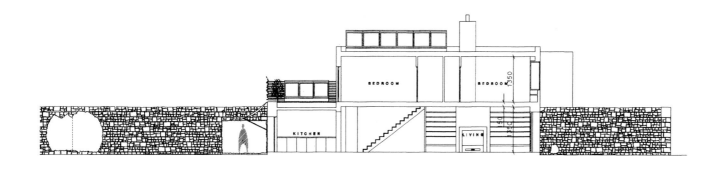

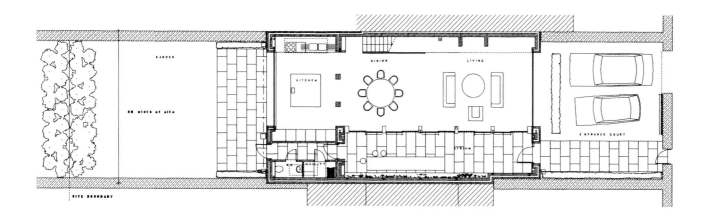

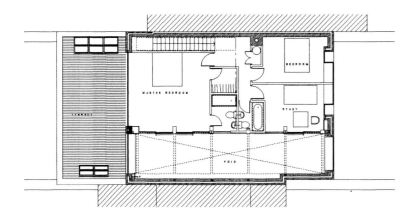

FROM ABOVE: Section; ground-floor plan;
first-floor plan; elevation to entrance court

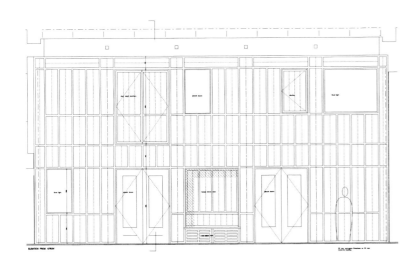

KOLATAN/MACDONALD STUDIO

OST/KUTTNER APARTMENTS

Vienna

This interior project (1997) was conceived as a form of miniature urbanisation. It consisted of three phases: identification of 'sites' within the existing space to act as locations for new structures; generation of these structures through cross-profiling; mapping of similarities using a method akin to co-citation mapping.

For the generation of the new structures on each site, section profiles of everyday domestic objects and furnishings were cross-referenced electronically, regardless of original scale and category, with an interest in registering the formal and operational similarities between them. Based on this information, they were then organised spatially and resurfaced.

The resulting structures are chimerical: the initial profiles as indexes of particular identities (bed, sink, sofa, etc) are now inextricably embedded within an entirely new entity, which they have helped produce. We will loosely refer to this new entity as a 'domestic scape', or synthetic topography.

The domestic scape, unlike the domestic space (the room), or the domestic object (the furniture), cannot be identified by categoric classification. Rather, like a particular landscape, its identification is contingent on the presence of a set of idiosyncratic features. As the discussion of identity is linked here to programmatic performance, it is useful to continue the landscape analogy in evaluating the synthetic topography. In the case of the bed, this would mean that a 'plateau' of

a certain measurement can be indentified as, but would not be limited to, a potential sleeping area. This is very different from the concept of a 'bed' or a 'bedroom', which are both categoric designations of identity, and therefore fixed in their programmatic associations.

The formal and programmatic conditions thus obtained are unknown and impossible to preconceive or predict. This excess of information poses an interesting problem in as much as it is ambiguous and therefore open to interpretation on many levels. The resulting synthetic topographies, unlike conventional subdivisions by rooms, do not register legible distinctions between spaces or programmes. The domestic scapes are always situated across the boundaries of the existing domestic spaces. The bed/bath scape, for example, forms a continuous surface within its own limits, a seamless transition between the space shaped by the 'bathtub' and the bedroom floor/wall. (A door into the 'bathtub' is sealed as the water level rises and presses against it.)

While the topographic model is useful in understanding certain aspects of these structures, it is important to note that the surface in this case is not just terrain, a top layer with a fairly shallow sectional relief, but deep – both conceptually and literally. Conceptually, this term is used to denote the possibility of an increased range. The surface is not exclusively thought of as thin, shallow, external etc,

but as capable of incorporating degrees of cavitation, thickness, interiority, three-dimensional space and so on. Considered in this way, the relationship between deep and shallow, space and surface, is not defined as a dichotomy, but within the terms of transformation. It is this capacity of the scape to change incrementally and continously that produces a chimerical condition between furniture, space and surface.

Conventional assumptions about the codification of the interior surfaces as floors, walls and ceilings do not always hold here. At the very least, the place and manner in which these elements meet is redefined.

In the final phase of the project, these individual scapes are interconnected across the space of the apartment in a manner similar to co-citation mapping (electronic literary indexing). This kind of similarity mapping yields both an analysis of already existing relationships by indicating the co-presence of certain idiosyncracies across, or regardless of, type, as well as a relational method of production that produces simultaneous effects across an established network.

An electronic web of second-iteration sites is constructed with the intention of mapping similarities and differences between previously unrelated entities. The individual sites are bound together as a system in which small-scale manipulations affect changes throughout varying scales and locales.

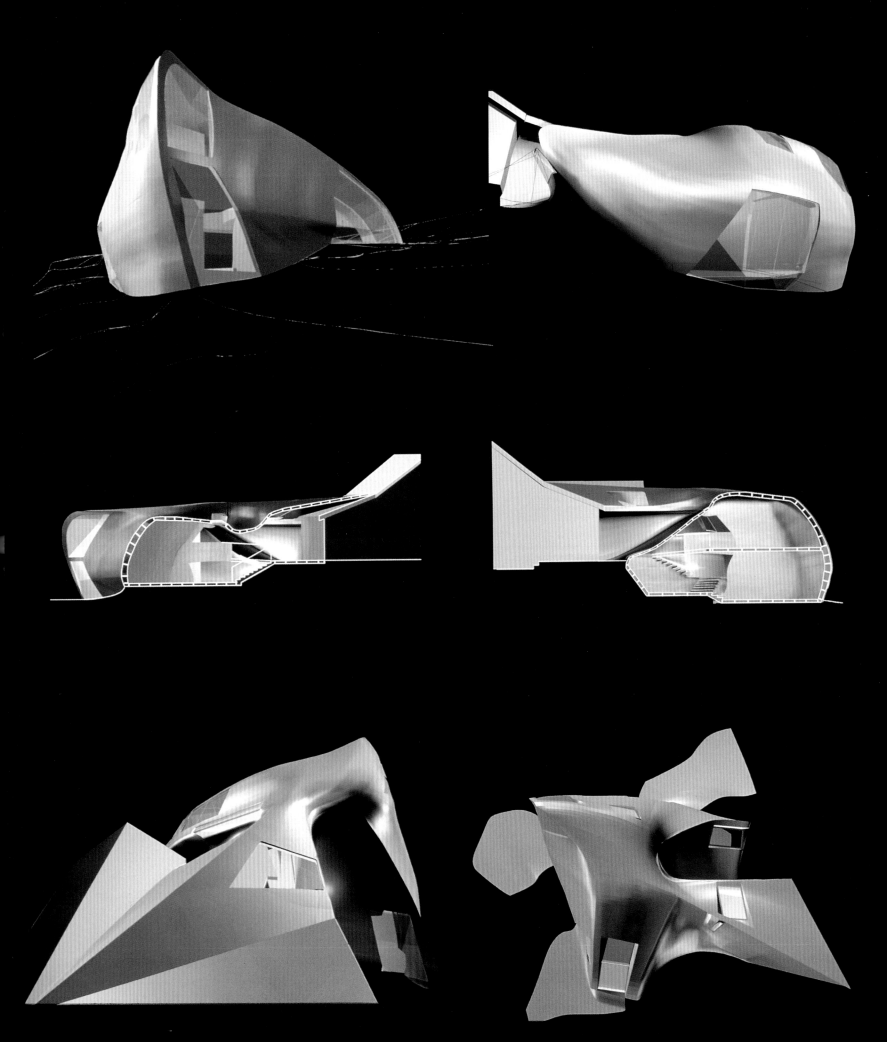

KOLATAN/MACDONALD STUDIO

RAYBOULD HOUSE ADDITION

Sherman, Connecticut

This project explores the potential of a hybrid architecture. The computer's specific capacity to map similarities across different categories while performing transformative operations is crucial to its conceptual and physical production.

For the design of this 'weekend home' addition, completed in 1998, information has been culled from the existing house, the landscape and the car. Their respective protocols and structural and spatial identities were electronically cross-referenced and systemically transformed into the new house.

The brief was to provide a 150-square-metre addition to the existing house, primarily used by the New York-based client to entertain guests. The new extension consists of two adjoining living areas, two bathrooms, and two bedrooms.

The 5.5 acre site is a gently sloping, 'pie-shaped', wooded parcel of land adjacent to an intersection on the south, a roadway on the east and farmlands to the west and north. The area of the compound includes a stream (with dam), which splits the site nearly in half along its longitudinal axis; two existing 17th-century structures (a 150-square-metre house and a 370-square-metre barn); a kidney-shaped, 1950s swimming pool and a small entry bridge.

The entry drive is on the eastern-most boundary of the site, running perpendicular to the stream. The immediate site of the addition is on the north-eastern side of the existing house. In this area, the landscape slopes some 30 per cent from west to east. The site drops sharply at the rear of the existing house, creating a 2.5-metre differential between the plateau on which the existing house rests and the lowest ground level of the new addition on its most eastern facade.

As a result of the project's proximity to a wetlands area, the addition had to be located no less than 23 metres from the top of the stream's bank. The structure's entire height could not exceed 10.5 metres.

The three-dimensional geometry of the building has been developed as an

'open-net shell'. This faceted structure is comprised of varying lengths and thicknesses of wood, which were calculated and designed by consulting engineers through structural analysis on a computer. The joinery of the wood members utilises a metal box that typically receives four struts in each of the intersection points of the faceted structure (not unlike a geodetic system). The double membrane panels are sheathed by rubber-cored plywood, which allows for the double-curving surface.

Most of the interior of the shell is finished in Philippine mahogany-veneered, rubber-cored plywood. The bathroom

walls and floors are mainly tiled. The exterior, waterproof membrane is covered in a custom-tailored, reinforced-thermoplastic membrane with hot-air welded seams. The window mullions continue the faceted structure.

For drainage purposes the window and door openings (along with their deflector and gutter systems) are strategically placed in the flattest surfaces of the structure. The mechanical systems are central air-conditioning and radiant-slab heating. All other flooring is carpeted.

OPPOSITE: Computer-generated images of exterior and sections; BELOW: Site plan

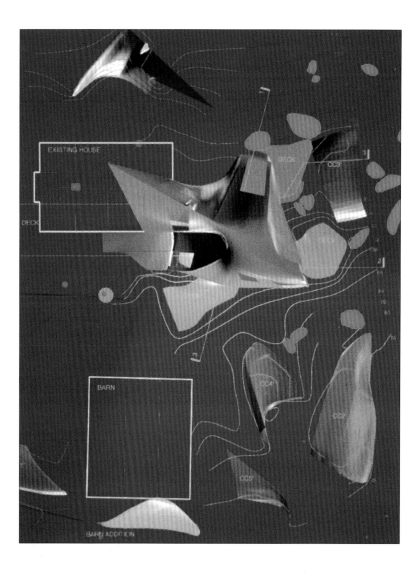

FROM ABOVE: Section; view from north east

BEN NICHOLSON
LOAF HOUSE

The Loaf House was originally planned for a site at 31st and Prairie Avenue in Chicago, where there had once been a turreted Victorian mini-mansion. Deflected by a technological squall, the house retrenched itself into the maybe world of cyberspace. Today, it is entirely digital and beneath its surface is a hypertext that leads into the quandaries and preoccupations of contemporary American domestic life.

Viewed within cyberspace, the Loaf House appears to be a brightly glowing, vapid nonentity. As one gets closer, it gathers focus to resemble a squared-off peg, hammered deep into the ground. Its ethereal appearance soon materialises into an accretion of gravity-bound things – some hanging, others thrusting upwards, and all inextricably linked.

Four looming, 10.5-metre towers, dedicated respectively to liquid, power-source, dirt and micro-airwave, push up through the innards of the building, extending citrus-yellow beams. These hover in the air, dangling rods from their tips, which support the facades like marionettes.

The facades

The end facades of the house 'fill-in' this dangling structure, giving the building the appearance of a tightly plugged tunnel. It is a tense structure, the perfect antidote to the weekly juggle of Saturday-morning soccer and after-school piano lessons for the kids. The east facade is a diaphragm of glassy shards, like a curtain of splinters. At the west end, a full protuberance pokes out of the glassy wall to form a well-rounded nose. And whenever a 'nose' makes itself felt, the spectre of a head is always suggested.

Viewing the south facade, overlooking the street, the observer's eyes must work fast, nipping about from place to place, roaming over the full panorama of the wall, finding clues about the experience of a day spent in the Loaf House.

In times gone by, such a facade might have sported an ornamental splendour of carved-stone *putti*, perched upon the leading edge of the wall. But this one opens itself to mechanical intervention: it is a spectrum of overt and latent forces, linked to the raw elements and to the activity of people within the house. It is criss-crossed with signs of movement, each caused by an activity known only to those inside.

Throughout the year, a substantial concrete cylinder moves sporadically up and down the wall. Sometimes it is wound tight against the supporting pulley, set high in the wall, at others it dangles low in its basket near the ground. Mostly, it slides back and forth against the markings, taking the temperature of some unknown virus inside the house. No one outside is privy to the logic of this public oscillation.

Above the house, a dull, flapping noise emanates from a crimson flag, billowing out from the edge of the roof. The flag flies only on certain days, no doubt when something worth celebrating is happening inside the house. Just below it are the blades of a windmill. When the actions of a windmill and a flag are seen side by side, the chore of one becomes the liberation of the other. The windmill appears to express curiosity as to why the flag is let loose to crack in the wind, doing nothing but announcing its freedom. The flag, in turn, seems surprised to see the hardened cycle of repetition reiterated over and again by the windmill. The sails of the windmill are mounted on a stumpy axle protruding from the facade. Its curvaceous blades flop round and round in the lake wind, turning an arbor connected to something deep within the house.

The entrance way

The front door and the postcard-sized kid's room are set into the east facade's sea of glass shards. The kid's room is at the nexus of the house, surveying the majority of the activities going on inside and out. A boxy hidey-hole sticks out in front of the glass facade, scaled to that famous space 'beneath the stairs' that shuts darkness in and grown-ups out. The front door is reached by a collection of steps that leads to a pivoted door, seemingly approaching and receding simultaneously. Its dense weight makes it look as if it is stranded in the glass facade. It is not so much an entrance to the house, as a weighted impediment to match the gravity of the place. Once through the door, the visitor is led into a tiny vestibule, lorded over by a caged balcony that is part of the kid's room.

Conglomeroom

Beyond the vestibule is a tall, compressed space called the Conglomeroom, a grand admixture of kitchen, dining room, living room and study. It is punctuated by the four towers that sustain the house and is lit by a trickling of lights, to which the eyes need time to adjust. One's fingers skirt over every surface, stopping to extract the secrets of the house by tapping into the hypertext lurking beneath its patina.

The kitchen is wrapped in a veneer of hyperlinked websites, probing the American preoccupation with food, drink and sanitation. Not only does a monitor above the stove offer up thousands of recipes from around the world, but virtual bacteria can be inspected when a fly lands on the plates drying above the sink. Nearby, the dining table is set for ten people culled from the nation's suburbs, selected for their normality. Behind the dining table is a shelved library, jammed with stacks of websites revealing metasystems, generic information, and the classical categories of knowledge established by Aristotle.

Basement

The basement is a collection of subterranean adventures that are best not spoken about too much, but are always loved and remembered. Down here is the pool-table, sauna box, and a repository for books – attached by a book wheel to the study above.

Angst Collector

The Angst Collector is a thin, undulating copper plate that forms the upper floor of the Loaf House, the sound-board for the cathartic life within the house, where the Loafers put up their feet and relax. It is drenched in history: its metal is taken from the copper wiring pulled from a B-52 bomber, which formerly conducted the millions of messages that kept the craft afloat. The metal is beaten flat by the collective memory of a whole city, replacing the brittle angst of citizens with the ring of a million hammer blows, a metallic choir for militaristic endeavour.

Vertical garden

The upper floor is accessed either via a staircase set into the south

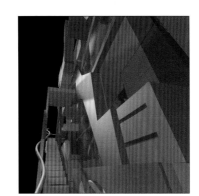

choreographed by the constant adjustments of the manipulatory webmasters around the world.

When the bedroom is vacant, a sundial pin, set into the conical funnel above the bed, guards time on sunny days, casting a temporal shadow that exists in a quiet vacuum.

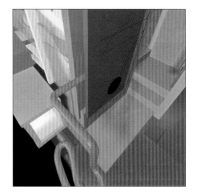

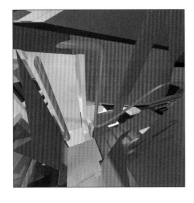

wall, or by way of a compound stairway embedded in the north wall. This wall is a vertical upended garden, a 2-metre-thick band of materiality, threaded with every sort of step and fireman's pole to give a sense of the true grace and vertigo experienced when going up and down.

An orange handrail winds its way between the structure, lancing the house as it passes the children's room and the Angst Collector and peeking into the fleshy sweetness of the bathroom. It then goes on through a portal to the outside, to an upper balcony that overlooks the bedroom.

Bedroom

The bedroom, which shares a peek-a-boo glass wall with the shower-stall next door in the bathroom, is a place that enhances the realm of horizontality. Above the queen-sized bed (a 4:3 ratio celebrated in antiquity) hovers a conic funnel leading to the sky. In here bodies can knot themselves in a frenzy or lay out flat to snag dreams, restore health and defragment their brains in readiness for the next day's onslaught. The mouse can scurry about the bedroom, peering into cupboards that are pregnant with the stuff of adornment: mysteries

The views beyond

The views from the Loaf House windows lead out to all manner of contextual websites. Worldwide weather can be tapped; cameras on sites across the world can be peered through, and the terra firma of Indian Country beneath the house can be prodded for content. Up above the house is an extensive roof terrace. Chicago takes special pleasure in its summer evenings, and there is no better place to gaze across the even landscape than from the flat rooftops of its housing stock. The roof is designed for spectator sport, and has all manner of appendages to view the

streetscape below and the incoming clouds above. Running the entire length of the house are five skinny skylights that reveal slices of the life inside the house. Residents can climb up onto a tractor seat, set onto the top of the western tower, and gaze across the prairie and the scorched-earth city

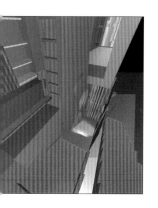

lots. Peering out from this perch provides the opportunity to put things in perspective. The view below offers a seamless grid of houses, each bursting with life and seemingly placed there to provide one with the outlook beyond one's own domain. Above, passing aircraft smear contrails across the sky, triggering our desire to be somewhere new and leaving us with just a thread of smoke to remind us where we stand.

The CD-Rom of the Loaf House is available to the savvy digital traveller and the voyeurist couch potato alike; it even provides a degree of handicap access for the digitally challenged. It is a cheap way for a thousand owners to roam about in an alternative realm, waving to their neighbours as they groan under the weight of the million-dollar mortgages that encapsulate the stuff of reality.

OPPOSITE AND ABOVE:
Walk-through vertical
garden of north wall;
RIGHT, FROM ABOVE:
South facade; kid's
room; CD-Rom pages

ROBERT HARVEY OSHATZ

MIYASAKA RESIDENCE

Obihiro, Japan

Whether one sees the Miyasaka Residence as an American or a Japanese house, it is my hope that it will evoke a feeling of naturalness, comfort and beauty.

Its naturalness stems from the fact that the structure is a poetic translation of its site and occupants. It is comfortable because it uniquely solves the occupants' functional needs and, equally, their spiritual requirements. It is beautiful in the sense that it will continue to reveal new surprises, mystery and delight – those elements that make architecture rewarding to its occupants for a lifetime.

Now that it is completed, I hope that the clients can say: 'If I were an architect, this is what I would have designed'.

Robert Harvey Oshatz

This single-family residence was built in 1997 on a 2.4 acre, wooded site in the heart of Obihiro, Japan. A farming and industrial centre with a population of over 170,000, Obihiro is located on the island of Hokkaido in the Tokachi district.

The Miyasaka family has lived on this parcel of land for many years. In 1994 they decided to build a new residence with modern conveniences. To achieve this goal, they commissioned Robert Harvey Oshatz, an American architect, to create a design reflective of the site, the family's unique programmatic needs, and their standing in the community.

The result of this partnership is an exquisite 700-square-metre, two-storey structure. The home's first floor is primarily devoted to private spaces for the Miyasaka elders, in addition to the family's community living areas. The second floor contains the master-bedroom suite and guest rooms.

At the outset of the project, a decision was taken to make significant use of materials supplied in the United States. The tremendous amount of prefabricated components dictated unusually close co-ordination between the architect and contractor. Additionally, this project was constructed on a fast-track schedule. In order to circumvent the significant costs and delays involved in shipping numerous construction documents back and forth across the Pacific, all of the drawings were done on a CAD system, and the files sent via the Internet.

In many respects, the process was a transcultural experiment for architect, client, and contractor. It was a pilot project to build a foundation of understanding and to explore a new way of doing business within the context of rapidly expanding technological possibilities.

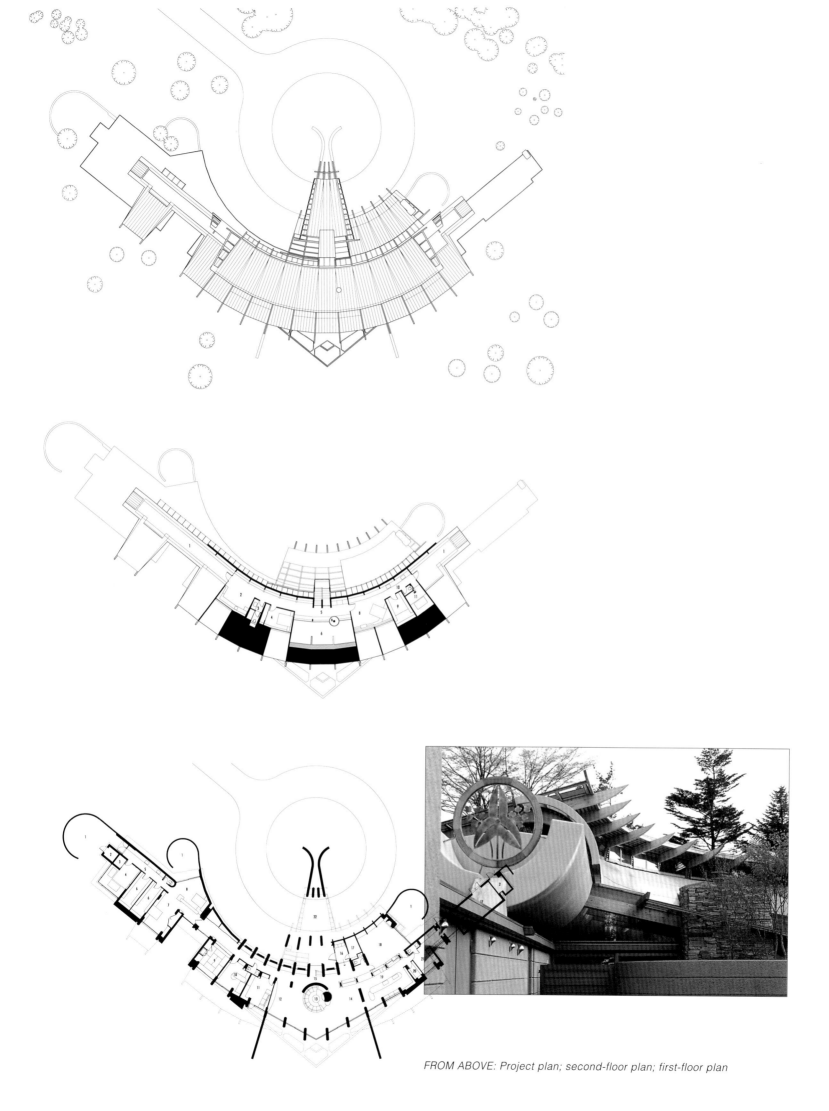

FROM ABOVE: Project plan; second-floor plan; first-floor plan

79

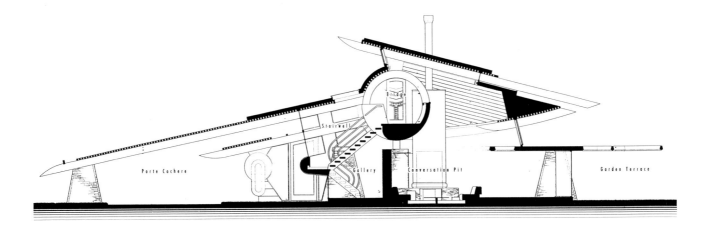

Section through entrance

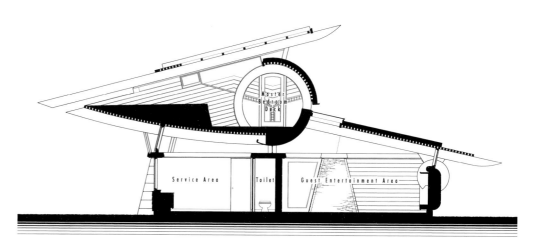

Section through stairwell

SETH STEIN ARCHITECTS
MEWS HOUSE WITH DOUBLE-DECK CAR LIFT
London

In 1994, Seth Stein Architects received a commission to build a new house on a tiny rectangle of land in a Knightsbridge mews. The project was completed in July 1997. Its brief was to provide the ultimate in flexible accommodation for a young couple, and the entire area of the site, approximately 6 x 8 metres, was excavated to provide the maximum space.

The owner's collection of vintage cars was central to the design. Elevating the idea of the car as an object of display, the house provides a showroom setting that is capable of storing a vehicle at the main living-level, below ground, and at street level.

The bottom car deck is a steel frame inset with Perspex panels. In a process similar to that adopted by the aviation and motor industries, these are finished with a sprayed silicone compound to prevent scratching from grit.

When raised, the transparent floor reveals a further level at the base of the hydraulic lift that provides a living-space linked to the main dining/living area. The transparent floor deck provides natural light from ground level and even a view to trees beyond the site, as well as continuing the view upwards over a distance of 6.5 metres. Landings are also glass, in order to transmit the maximum natural light throughout.

The upper car deck is finished in limestone and fits snugly into the space so that upon entering there is no indication that it is capable of being raised – like an aircraft carrier deck.

There is, of course, the option in both decks to use the space without cars, at which time these areas become calm, somewhat austere living accommodation.

The sense of space and dynamics is heightened when one explores the potential created by a house that rearranges itself internally. For instance, friends arrive at ground-floor level in a space with a transparent floor, lit from below. When dinner is served, instead of going down by way of the continuous glass-and-steel staircase, the hydraulics can deliver the party silently to the next stage of the evening. After dinner, the lift pit may be activated by raising the deck once more, providing living-room seating.

From the street, this house seems conventional enough, with a few discreet touches of high-tech, minimal detailing. It is inside where the fun starts.

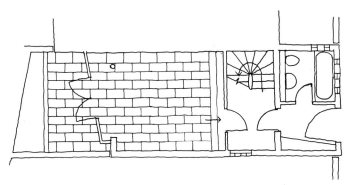

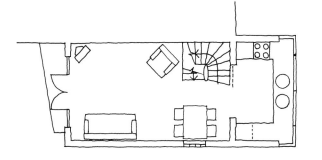

CHANCE DE SILVA ARCHITECTS

DES-RES VENUS: STUDIO-HOUSE, CINEMA, GALLERY AND LOVE HOTEL
London

Venus was always des, but only eventually res. Why did this little house take so long to become a home?

When Graham Cooper, financial journalist and art provocateur, expressed interest in working on an architectural project, Chance de Silva invited him to collaborate on developing a small site in Highbury, North London. Venus was the name of a garment factory that once operated from a rickety shed on the site, fast becoming a picturesque ruin.

The practice had visited the offices of Tadao Ando and Shin Takamatsu in Japan, and many of their smaller constructions in Osaka and Kyoto. These modern buildings occupy space in ways that are influenced by the *machiya*, the city houses of traditional Kyoto architecture. The new Venus, it was decided, would address the street in a similar way. The building was designed to be private and defensive at street level but to open up internally, especially at a higher level, to let in light and create views. Modern Japanese dwellings by Ando, Toyo Ito and others often conform to this organisational schema whilst projecting a radically different aesthetic. This would also be true of Venus.

Another useful notion for a small building, borrowed from Japan, is the variable occupation of space, not just in the flexible use of domestic rooms but in the ideological sense that even a compact building can be many things. For example, some of Cooper's ambitions were integrated within the project. He prompted the idea of utilising Venus as a small cinema. In the building, this is manifested in steps the full width of the studio room, which make two rows of stalls behind the 'pit' of the lowered floor. An involved client-partner, Cooper also recorded his daily observational role during the construction period by taking a photograph at 8.45 each morning. In an ironic take on the work of Douglas Gordon, or the Paul Auster scripted film, *Smoke*, he made his snapshots into the video *3-Minute Venus*, screened in the 'cinema'.

For the exterior of the building, the preference was for a naturally weathered material, with an appearance that would continue to evolve. The original Venus shed was red, and the desire was to return colour to the street with the new building. The model of the proposed construction was conceived as a tiny paperweight of mottled copper on top of a heavy wooden base, like a balcony corner post of the *Kiyomizudera* temple. In the building itself, above the solid base of recycled bricks, the envelope is a well-insulated timber frame clad in post-patinated copper. Parts of this shell were prefabricated and delivered by crane.

Cooper's work also took him sporadically to Japan, and the idea of a reciprocal stop-over for vistors to London became attached to the small, modern folly emerging as the Venus project. Already aptly named, Venus became like a Japanese love-hotel. The idea of the love-hotel is not translatable into that of the Western brothel. In Japan's tiny homes, often lived in by extended families, and with small, multi-use rooms and literally paper-thin walls, even a married couple might choose to find privacy outside the home.

Oddly, this idea meshed with a more esoteric preoccupation. During the design stage, the practice had been intrigued by a theory that all of Shakespeare's mature dramas are built on a plot template first constructed in the narrative poem *Venus and Adonis*. The question was how this theoretical framework might be applied to architecture, perhaps over a sequence of projects. One aspect of the myth of Venus represents the dual personality of woman – most directly in her sexual aspect (on the one hand objectified, idealised and chaste, on the other, instinctive, natural and active). This dual aspect can also represent broader concepts such as the rational/irrational divide of left/right-side brain activity, which, in an architectural analogy, encompasses the functional/non-functional dilemma contained in every architectural decision. In this

FROM ABOVE: The original Venus; interior, Takayama; model; OPPOSITE FROM ABOVE, L TO R: Street views; patinated-copper prefabricated side panel delivered by crane; ground-floor plan; first-floor plan

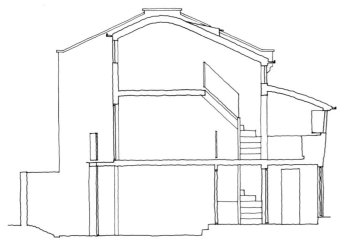

*ABOVE: Living room looking towards kitchen;
section; RIGHT: Light-box from Frank Watson's
Interior World*

project, decisions were nudged in the less rational direction – the direction, incidentally, of the Eastern principle. Like its predecessor, Venus looks utterly unlike anything else in the street.

As a further elaboration on this idea, two artists were invited to collaborate on the final stages of Venus. Their work would provoke questions and explore tangents that might not naturally arise from functional considerations. Frank Watson, for example, took advantage of the fact that Venus is an enclosure animated by the play of light. His series of light-boxes entitled *Interior World* take the building as a context for explorations into photography, spiritualism, architecture and light.

The artist Matt Hale developed a connection between the architectural themes and his work with liquid sculptures. He placed a 'stained-glass' window of glass tubes, filled with coloured domestic fluids (shampoo, detergent etc) in front of the glass block *shoji*. He also exposed the drain (where all domestic chemicals escape into the environment), and his glass welcome mat is immediately inside the front door.

So Venus became a public gallery. The white-walled spaces were sparsely furnished with just enough clues to indicate the domestic functions of each area. The industrial use of the former building was also continued in a studio-workshop space, effectively defining the planning use as 'live-work'. In-between curatorial duties for the exhibition, this monastic studio room was used as a workspace. It opens onto the Zen calm of the hundred terracotta pots that constitute the garden.

Venus was completed in 1998, and at last, will become occupied as a house. Fitting and furnishing Venus to accommodate the untidiness of living is the final stage before des-Venus enjoys the delayed gratification of res-Venus.

FROM ABOVE: Light-box from Frank Watson's Interior World; *Matt Hale's 'stained-glass' window (detail); Matt Hale's artwork revealing drain*

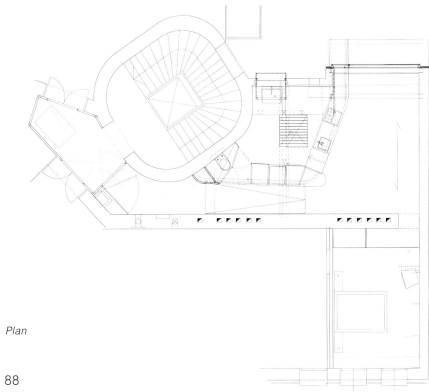

Plan

EICHINGER ODER KNECHTL

MONOCOQUE, SCHRETTER APARTMENT
Vienna

Completed in May 1998, this former laundry attic room has been converted into a 35-square-metre, fully equipped loft. Apart from the separate 15-square-metre bedroom, all basic functions are housed in a 'multi-directional unit'.

One wall has been removed and the roof structure has been covered with metal and plasterboard. Additionally, part of the exterior garret wall has been replaced with a large, two-part, moveable glass construction.

Inside the heavy metal, front security door is a large cupboard covered with 'ferrari' net, which acts as a translucent room-divider and houses the washing machine and control unit for all functions within the loft, operable by remote control. In the evening it transforms into a huge lamp.

The lavatory is located at one end of the cupboard, separated by stainless-steel doors that allow access from both sides. These can be closed in front of the lavatory pan so that it disappears into its own storage unit, hidden in a tiny space and leaving a path through the cupboard. Alternatively, a larger, luxurious space can be created.

The path through the cupboard allows access to the kitchen, which is lined by a net wall on one side and the cupboard on the other. Behind the net is the sink, enclosed in a glass cube. The net wall can be folded to create a shower cubicle, its fittings concealed and integrated into a metal column. In the shower area, the black 'sickaflex' gaps in the American oak yacht floor have been routed to form a water drain. An electrically operated window in the roof is located directly above the shower, so that the occupant can also wash directly in the snow or rain. Once the net wall is folded the other way, the shower and sink are concealed, leaving no clue that they exist. It is therefore possible to allow snow to enter the room, creating a particular ambience for certain occasions.

The kitchen itself consists of one, single unit which also extends outside the building. Inside, it is made of oak, outside, of concrete, with a small recessed herb garden.

The large, two-part window is electrically operated. Part one is a studio window, which tilts upwards until it reaches a height of 2.10 metres. Part two is a balustrade window, operated separately, which slides outside along the concrete unit, creating a balcony space that extends the size of the room.

The heating and all windows, lights and doors are operated centrally via the control unit, which can be accessed by telephone.

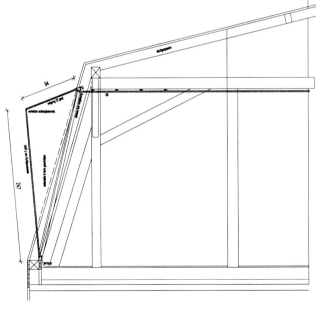

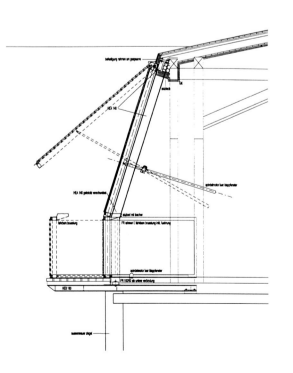

LEFT TO RIGHT: Sections of windows, parts 1 and 2

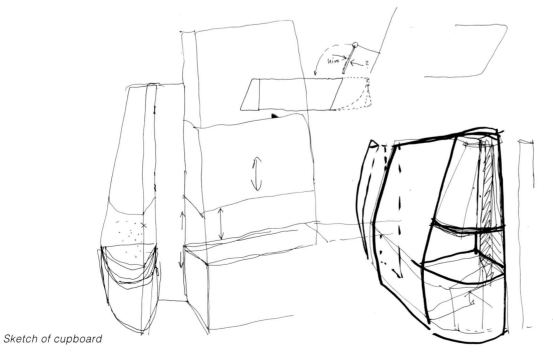

Sketch of cupboard

MATTHEW PRIESTMAN ARCHITECTS/PHILLIP TEFFT

MEWS HOUSE
London

The American owner of this double mews house in Belgravia chose it for its discreet sophistication in a central area, wishing to convert it into a contemporary home.

The freeholder, Grosvenor Estates, was inflexible concerning proposed modifications to the exterior fabric, which were eventually confined to two rooflights, a new entrance door and the replacement of timber-framed and glazed fenestration. An existing internal garage adjacent to the entrance had to be retained.

Completed in 1998, the house uses an inverted section as its programme, with guest/children's bedrooms and adjacent lounge located on the ground floor, generous entertaining spaces on the first floor, and a private suite on the second floor.

The three levels are linked by an open *scala regia* stair occupying a transitional zone of entrance, passage and vertical movement with a glass bridge connection. Animated by natural and artificial light, it reveals the full height of the house.

Voids containing storage space, cloakroom and cupboards for audio/visual equipment provide a clear visual and functional orientation as a dominant theme. This statement is enhanced by a narrow rooflight combined with back-lit light-boxes and directional lighting, placed in relation to the reconfigured sash windows of the original external wall. It is contradicted, however, by the specific interruptions of the kitchen enclosure, the edge-of-void benching and a top-floor dressing room.

The living room overlaps the stair and is directly and perpendicularly connected to the dining area with terrace beyond. This 'L' plan within an overall 10 x 10 metre footprint is completed by a kitchen area as a knuckle of activity, partly connected to and separable from dining and living room, with sliding panels and screen reinforcing a dynamic open plan. The first-floor plan is thus neither an open-plan arrangement, nor compartmentalised; an ambivalent state of overlapping and communication is intended.

The sinuous sequence of private rooms on the second floor – the study overlooking the stair, the main bedroom and the final privacy of the bathroom – is reflected in movement through spaces at first and ground floor.

Materials are restrained: limestone throughout the ground floor; oak for the upper floors, stairs and battened top ceiling; slate in the upper bathroom; timber benching and wardrobes accentuated by aluminium, stainless-steel and coated mild-steel metals. Off-white predominates as a wall and ceiling tone, broken only by a single synthetic colour to the entrance door.

The stair zone, dissolved compartmentalisation, and non-axial movement, motivated by a wish for coherent and seamless transformation, provide a struc-ture that articulates the complexity of living. The given conditions of a mews-type house, exacerbated by reactionary aesthetic control, are modified into a contemporary interior.

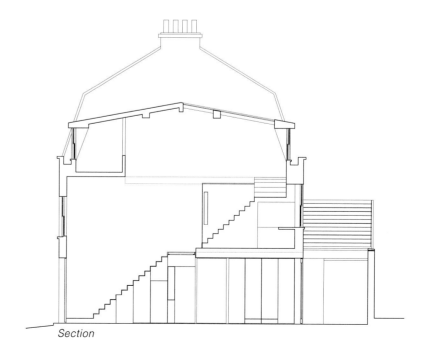

Section

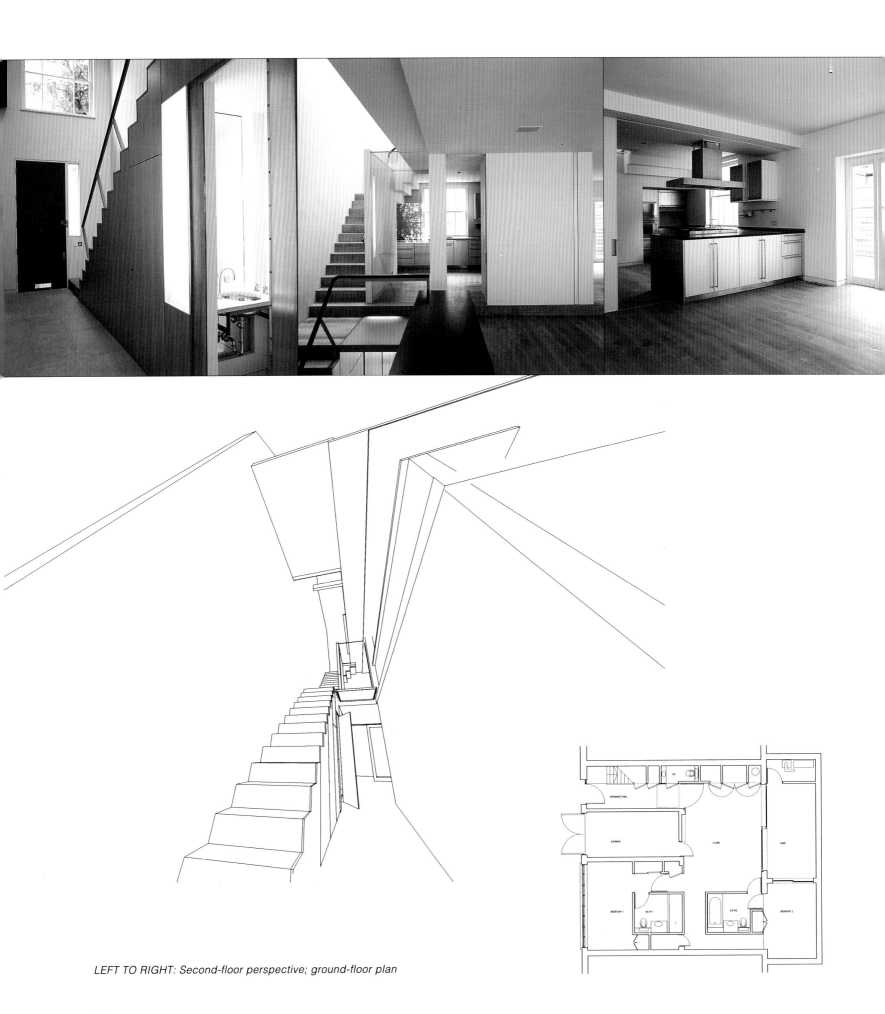

LEFT TO RIGHT: Second-floor perspective; ground-floor plan

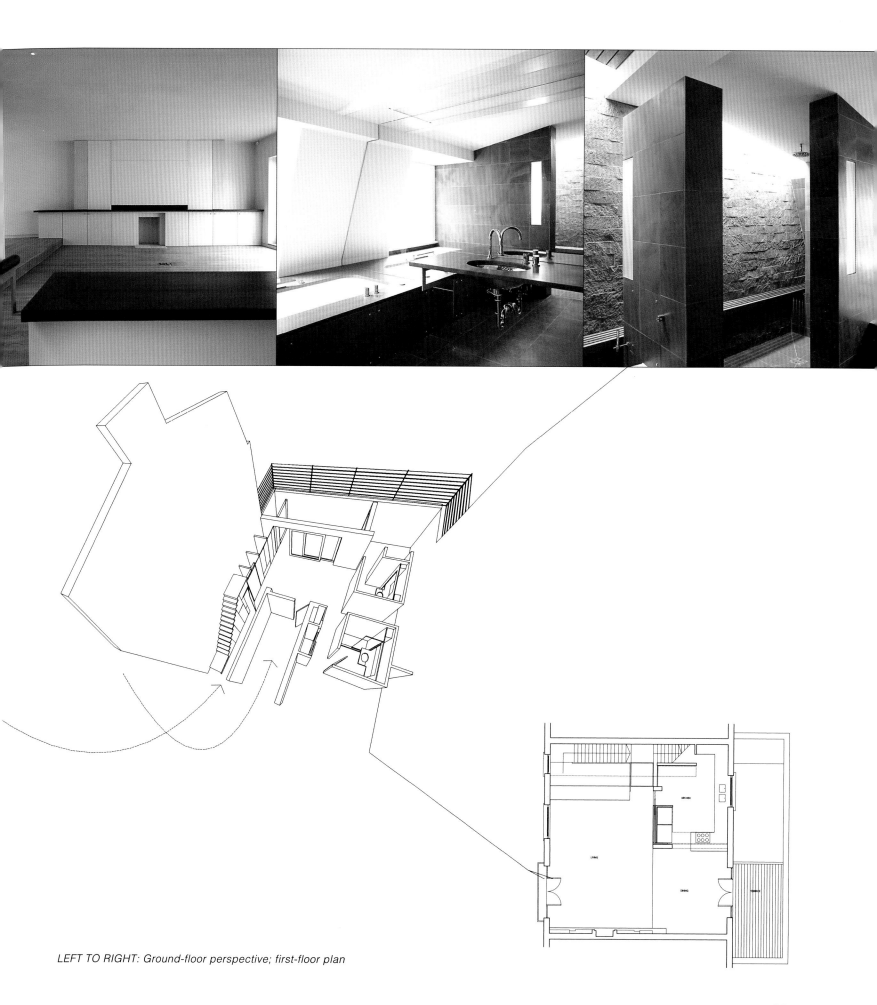

LEFT TO RIGHT: Ground-floor perspective; first-floor plan

BIOGRAPHIES

De Blacam and Meagher Architects was formed in 1976. Shane de Blacam is a graduate of UCD and the University of Pennsylvania. He has worked with Chamberlain, Powell and Bon, and Louis I Kahn. John Meagher, a graduate of Bolton Street, has collaborated with Wallace McHarg Roberts and Todd, Venturi Rauch and Scott Brown.

Alberto Campo Baeza is Chairman and Professor of Design at Madrid University. His buildings include the houses Turegano, Garcia Marcos and Gaspar. He has recently completed the 'Porta dei Fiori' in San Dona di Piave in Venice and is currently constructing a bank headquarters in Granada and high-tech offices in Mallorca, both first-prize winners in open competitions.

Helen Castle is a writer and freelance editor who lives in London. She has an MSc in the History of Modern Architecture from the Bartlett School of Architecture. Currently she is writing a book about modern houses for Academy Editions.

Chance de Silva Architects consists of Stephen Chance and Wendy de Silva. Both were trained at the Bartlett and now work separately in private practice. Following several joint architectural commissions, Venus was conceived as the first in a series of self-initiated projects that involve teaming up with non-architects.

Decoi Architects was established in Paris in 1991 as a design studio. Their first architectural commissions followed a period of teaching at the AA. These were located all over the world, reflecting Decoi's diverse ethnic backgrounds and international portfolio. They have developed a new model of nomadic, flexible architecture, facilitated by bases in Paris and Kuala Lumpur and state-of-the-art technology.

Eichinger Oder Knechtl was formed in the early 1980s as a partnership encompassing practitioners from a range of disciplines from science to graphic design. Stefan Eichinger and Christian Knechtl met whilst studying architecture in Vienna.

Future Systems was founded in 1979 by Jan Kaplicky and David Nixon, and is now directed by Jan Kaplicky and Amanda Levete. The practice aims to create work that is innovative and provocative, and which challenges traditional preconceptions of space.

Mark Guard Architects was established in 1986 and specialises in housing. After studying at the University of Toronto and the Royal College of Art, Guard worked for Richard Rogers, Rick Mather and Eva Jiricna. In 1997 the practice received the RIBA Award for Houses and Housing.

Kolatan/MacDonald Studio was founded in 1986 by Sulan Kolatan and William J MacDonald. The firm's award-winning work can be found in the permanent collections of the Museum of Modern Art, New York, the San Francisco Museum of Modern Art and the Avery Library Collection. Their projects have also been exhibited widely in museums and galleries.

Enric Massip-Bosch studied at the ETSAB-UPC, becoming Professor of its Architecture Design Department in 1994. He established EMB-Estudi D'Arquitectura in 1996 with Horacio Espeche and Joan Sabate. EMB has won several competitions currently under construction and is researching new possibilities in architecture. Massip-Bosch has worked with Marta Mas on several projects; Casa Cabrils is their latest collaboration.

Ben Nicholson was educated at the AA and Cranbrook. He teaches at IIT, Chicago. His 'Thinking the Unthinkable House' is a CD-Rom about the B-52 bomber, Michelangelo and Geometry. Other projects include the Loaf and Appliance Houses. He is currently writing a book about the Laurentian Library.

Francis Nordemann is a French architect and urbanist practising in Paris. He has designed several major projects including housing, educational buildings, religious institutions, recreational and health facilities. His firm is involved in urban design studies and projects around Europe. He is currently Head of the School of Architecture of Normandy University.

Robert Harvey Oshatz, Architect was established in 1971 in Oregon, Portland. The company has provided a wide variety of architecture – both commercial and residential – planning, interior design and construction management services for developers and individuals. Oshatz has acted as a construction manager and builder on a number of projects and is a guest lecturer for the Smithsonian Institute's Continuous Architecture series.

Matthew Priestman Architects has been involved in a range of projects including strategic masterplanning, urban design, cultural facilities, higher education, residential and contemporary interiors. Priestman formed the practice in 1988. Previously he had worked with Chris Wilkinson and Will Alsop. He regularly lectures in Britain and abroad.

Pugh + Scarpa is based in Santa Monica, California. The partners have practised architecture together since 1985 and formed the partnership in 1988. It covers an extensive range of projects including custom residential design, replacement and new affordable housing. Gwynne Pugh is also a trained engineer, recognised as a leader in the field of seismic engineering and design.

Claudio Silvestrin was educated in Milan by AG Fronzoni, completing his studies in 1985 at the Architectural Association in London, where he still lives and works. He is known for his rigorous and elegant minimal architecture.

SITE is a New York-based architecture and environmental arts organisation, founded by James Wines 25 years ago. Wines has designed many projects, including art museums, commercial buildings, international exposition pavilions, restaurants and theme parks. The former Chair of Environmental Design at Parsons School of Design, he is the winner of many major art and design awards and has written several books.

Studio Granda is based in Reykjavík, Iceland and was established in 1987 by Margrét Haroardóttir and Steve Christer. The partners trained at Edinburgh and Newcastle Universities respectively and later graduated from the Architectural Association, London where they still teach. Notable works include the Reykjavík City Hall (1992), the Supreme Court of Iceland (1996) and the 'Aktion Poliphile' residence in Wiesbaden (1992).

Tanner Leddy Maytum Stacy Architects comprises James Tanner, William Leddy, Marsha Maytum and Richard Stacy. Founded in 1989, TLMS continues a professional association that began in the early 80s. The diverse body of work that has grown from this association reflects a combination of shared vision and individual interests.